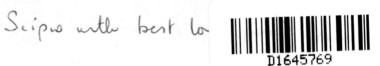

On Being Someone

A Christian Point of View

Helen Oppenheimer

imprint-academic.com

Published in the UK by
Imprint Academic, PO Box 200, Exeter EX5 5YX, UK

Published in the USA by
Imprint Academic, Philosophy Documentation Center
PO Box 7147, Charlottesville, VA 22906-7147, USA

ISBN 9781845402280

A CIP catalogue record for this book is available from the
British Library and US Library of Congress

Contents

To my great-grandson
REUBEN MOSLEY
who is much too young to read this book
but who I hope will
be pleased with it one day.

Preface

This book continues the discussions in *What a piece of work: on being human* (Imprint Academic 2006) and may be considered its sequel. I especially want to thank my husband, as ever; for all his help; and my three daughters and their families for all manner of encouragement. I owe specific thanks to: Ivo Mosley for benevolent appraisal; Xanthe Mosley for simplifying the title; Adam Scott for helping me to argue myself out of a dead end; Matilda King for information about medical ethics; Noah Mosley for keen friendly arguments; and my niece Patricia Brims for judicious advice at an early stage.

I should like to thank the Society for the Study of Christian Ethics, for helping a free-lance academic to keep in touch; and the parish of St Martin de Grouville and its Rector, Mike Lange-Smith, for providing a firm foundation for chapter 19. The late Gordon Dunstan keeps cropping up with gratitude, especially in chapter 6.

The numerous notes and the sketchy bibliographies represent my efforts to apply the maxim of a maths teacher long ago: 'Show your workings.' They may be taken as an optional extra, for the benefit of people who like looking things up and for people who find it annoying when they cannot look things up. I have indicated where I have been recapitulating and refurbishing ideas from earlier books now out of print. I am grateful to Anthony Freeman of Imprint Academic for coping doughtily with my footnotes and for providing a congenial reference on page 180.

Helen Oppenheimer

I. HUMANITY

Chapter 1

Who Are We?

What is man, that thou art mindful of him: and the son of man, that thou visitest him?

Psalm 8.4

Among all the creatures in the physical universe there are some who seem to be more than simply physical, because they are aware of being creatures in the universe. Though human beings essentially belong to the world of nature, and that is to be gladly emphasized, they still stand out as the most complex and fascinating of all living beings. Like and also unlike other animals, they respond to what happens to them; they make plans and carry them out; they recognize one another, sometimes lovingly; they make friends and enjoy their company; they shape the world around them for convenience and for delight; they ask questions both practical and theoretical; and many of them try to praise God.

The old enquiry 'What is man?' used to be a compact way of identifying our questions about human nature and human value, exerting ourselves to take thought about the status of human beings in the world. The enquiry now appears both sexist and 'speciesist' and cannot be expressed so neatly any more. 'What are human beings?' is more politically correct, but it seems to be almost pointless to ask it. We have a clear idea what human beings are and know a good deal about their biology and their history. The sorts of things we want to say about them are apt to be fairly straightforward. We can describe them in general and in particular and understand that in some ways they are like and in other ways not at all like one another. Even when people baffle us, that is a practical perplexity about how to deal with them, not a theoretical perplexity about understanding the world.

Yet there remain the fundamental questions which 'What is man?' used to raise, concerning how to think of humanity. The traditional problems about our nature, value, prospects, fears and hopes still need to be put into words. In a small book called *What a piece of work*,[1] I embarked on these problems by considering humankind as part of the natural universe which Christians believe God set in motion, asking how human beings stand among other creatures and how they are to be valued,

There comes a time for leaving aside comparisons with our fellow creatures in order to attend to our own experience. It makes a good start to think of myself as a human animal, but then what does it mean to be a person, to be counted as *someone*? The question 'What is man?' turns into 'Who are we?' We do not have to be especially perplexed by the particular human beings around us to be impressed by the peculiar fact that conscious experience is a feature of the universe.

George is a straightforward sort of person who is not given to hiding his feelings, so it is quite clear what is fretting him. We can tell that his finger is hurting. He is worrying that it may be septic. We can ask him where the pain is and he can show us the sore place. What he cannot show us is his worry. It is just as real as the inflammation, but where is it? Is it in his head? Even a brain surgeon could never find it, though anxiety may be giving George a physical headache. The brain surgeon could not even find the headache, however up-to-date his apparatus. Cells, even cells which hurt, are a different kind of thing from pains, even well-understood pains. We know what we mean by saying that George cannot have a headache unless he is conscious, but is his consciousness a sort of thing we could locate, and if so what sort of thing?

---

[1]   Oppenheimer (2006).

People are not obliged to go in for deep thinking about thought, but once they have begun they cannot simply stop. Hamlet announced that

> ... he that made us with such large discourse,
> Looking before and after, gave us not
> That capability and god-like reason
> To fust in us unused.[2]

Do we really know what it means to say that George is conscious? We know that as the dependable man he is, he is likely to behave in certain ways, but is his real self some-where, so to say, *behind* his characteristic behaving, hidden behind it out of our reach or even out of his reach?

Once we start asking these questions, comprehending what a person is does not seem so straightforward. The point of posing problems like this at the start of a small book about Christian theology is not to claim to offer thorough solutions, but to set up a frame of mind which does not always expect reductive commonsense to provide the whole answer. Suppose we find more things in heaven and earth than are dreamt of by philosophical self-assurance, it is worth looking into their meaning.

When people set about using their god-like reason for try-ing to understand the world, and especially when they hope to commend their thinking to scientists, they must recog-nize from the start that the truth is to be found out, not made up. Whether they are trying to discover what is causing a small pain or what the vast universe is really like, it is not good enough to say, 'Well, that's the way I see it.' They are required to look at whatever data there are objectively, from outside anyone's individual point of view. They must try to take what Thomas Nagel called 'The view from nowhere.'[3] But Nagel's paradox really is a paradox. Views are logically from viewpoints. If I make the effort, perhaps I can learn to disengage myself from my own particular situation and look at where I am from outside, but this scientific detach-

---

[2] *Hamlet*, IV. iv.
[3] See Nagel (1986).

ment has to be an achievement and is not to be taken for granted.

Whether it is the nature of the cosmos or my own nature which I am exploring, I may hope to win through to a just appreciation of reality; but I have to begin somewhere, not nowhere, in order to advance to anywhere else. That is, when I am considering what there really is I have to start looking from some point of view, restricted or far-reaching, high up or low down, ordinary or strange. I, myself, short-sighted or long-sighted as I may be, cannot simply be taken out of the whole picture, if there is any picturing going on. Just to say that *I* am looking at what the world is like draws attention to my own particular experience of looking, even if the ideal is supposed to be complete detachment.

Among all the things there are, we find that we must allow for ourselves, that is, for one sort of object which is not merely an object, a kind of thing which is not inert but mindful of other things. The curious basic notion of *awareness* is wrapped up in the data. When questions are asked and answers are given about what there is in the universe, the reality of consciousness and its strangeness must be taken into account.

When one considers how consciousness fits into the world of physics, puzzlement may lead to wonder; but the problem at first is an intellectual enquiry concerning facts rather than values, not yet an enquiry about spiritual realities. 'Consciousness' is a morally neutral concept which is roughly synonymous with 'awareness'. The vocabulary of 'inner' and 'outer' arises naturally for picking out the difference between a conscious being and an inanimate object.

There are plenty of possible complexities. A tree responds to its surroundings and is indeed a living thing, but we do not believe that a tree is aware of its surroundings. There are insect-eating plants which are called 'sensitive'. Words-worth declared his 'faith that every flower Enjoys the air it breathes' and there is no need to call this meaningless; but it would be confusing to take it prosaically. If what Words-worth meant was that trees and flowers were like people in literally having a subjective life, he was surely mistaken.

When a human being has tragically lost the capacity to have any experiences, people find the word 'vegetable' cruelly apt, because vegetable life is not conscious.

One can imagine a world with nobody in it, a world which simply goes on and on, which is never viewed nor considered nor understood, because there are no conscious beings to look at it or be puzzled by it or find out about it. Maybe that is what the universe was like for billions of years; but this mysterious item called consciousness has let in something new. The fact of consciousness means that there are some beings who are able to have experience of reality outside themselves, whatever realities there may turn out to be. I find that I am one of these beings.

Scientists in the course of their enquiries appropriately proceed to set aside the particular experience which belongs to me, and consider me objectively as a thing among things. I cannot repudiate the validity, the authority nor indeed the usefulness of such a scientific procedure, but as I live my life and call myself 'I', I must go on claiming that I am more than a thing, not only an object but a subject. Whether we are occupied with practical doing or with thoughtful knowing, our lives are founded on the dim or clear awareness each of us has of being someone.

To start with human conscious awareness by no means forbids people to take the animal creation into account. Most of us believe that animals are conscious and many of us are inclined to treat their consciousness as important.[4] Asserting that human beings are animals *and more,* people enquire into how much more and what kind of more. Some people look on some animals as persons, whatever answers they would give to questions about whether animals have rights. Other people still suppose that our fellow creatures do not matter much. There are enough of these people to make it obligatory to provide at the outset a plain indication of disagreement with them.

But the present concern is to start upon a different exploration, which leaves on one side the arguments about the

---

[4] See Oppenheimer (2006).

status and value of animals. Just as a human being is an animal *and more*: so in turn a conscious creature, human or animal, is a physical body and more. When we translate the old question 'What is man?' as 'Who are we?' we are beginning to ask distinctively human questions about what our notion of being 'someone' signifies. Taking our awareness of ourselves and one another to pieces and trying to put it together again is a characteristically human philosophical activity, a primary task for rational thought.

When I ask what 'someone' means, the example I must take is myself. I know what it means to be *me* by being me. 'I am someone', 'I am myself' and 'I am I' are tautologies. These sentences look like statements of fact, but they are peculiar statements, because they cannot be false and have to be true. Do they really give any information? They do give rise to intriguing philosophical questions about how a particular 'someone', this individual 'I' which seems to me at this moment to be such a clear idea, can be identified at different times and places as the same individual and distinguished as a different person from any other individual 'I'.

Once it is granted that *I* am more than this thing which is my body, what are the essential criteria which anyone can use for recognizing the particular continuing 'someone' who is the one I call *me*? The physical criteria are the most manageable but turn out not to capture the whole picture of what a person is. What I am like can be described in various ways, but how much of all this data is needed for me to be the same one and to go on being the same one? It is comprehensible to say that I, the person I am, might have become a lawyer although I made other choices, but does it make sense to say that I, my parents' baby, might have been a boy not a girl and still have been *me*? If I ask, Suppose that I had been a cat, or even a bat,[5] instead of a human being, what am I to try to imagine?

Is it fantasy or nonsense to tell a story about somebody turning into somebody else? Could an emperor take up residence in a body which has been shaped so far by the life of a

---

[5]   See Nagel (1979); Goodrich (1969) pp. 129–130.

peasant?[6] There are plenty of apparently coherent tales about people being turned into animals and vice versa. When human beings treat animals harshly, it is not unreasonable to ask, 'How would you like to be treated like that if *you* were a dog, or a horse, or a laboratory rat?' It seems that Buddhists responsibly envisage the idea that in another life, as a penalty for my misdoings, I may be reincarnated as a less fortunate creature.

But if I begin to explore what these notions could mean, it is not obvious that I could have been, or could become, some other creature and still be myself. Perhaps I might enter one day with my human memories into the experience of being a gorilla; but could there be anything left of *me,* living the life of a caterpillar? Where are we to draw the line which divides the conceivable from the inconceivable? Bernini sculpted Daphne turning into a laurel tree and we readily suspend disbelief, but when one sets about imagining Daphne's experience after her transformation, what one imagines is Daphne trapped *in* a tree, not Daphne alive *as* a tree. These sound like practical questions but are near the frontier of logical impossibility. One is inclined to think that such enquiries cannot have answers. Perhaps it is not a serious enterprise for human beings to ask this sort of philosophical question, but only an absorbing mind-stretching diversion like crossword puzzles.

But when the enquiries about what it means to be 'me' are shaped as moral problems concerning the way real people ought to live, then they come to life as questions which might have, and indeed urgently need, real answers.[7] When did the person who counts as *me* begin to exist, so that other people began to have duties to me?[8] Is an early embryo a person already? Has that man or that woman who has lapsed into a permanent coma ceased to exist? Is somebody who is now brain-dead a person still? Decisions about the

---

[6] See John Locke *Essay concerning human understanding* Book II Chapter XXVII paragraph 15; Williams (1973) pp. 11–12; Oppenheimer (1973) pp. 31–32.

[7] I have looked at some of these arguments in Oppenheimer (1989).

[8] See Ford (1988).

wrongness or rightness of abortion or euthanasia demand reflection about whether there is a *person* here and how such a person ought to be treated.

Many people go on further to ask, Is it responsible to hope that someone who really has died can inherit eternal life in another world?[9] They certainly feel as if they are asking a factual question about what is actually going to happen to them. The answers which people give, explicitly or implicitly, to questions like these about the presence or absence of persons make a difference to the way they live their lives.

Human beings characteristically puzzle about their own existence as mysterious and marvel at it as wonderful. The history of thought is even more likely to be oversimplified than the history of events, but certainly people have had notions about themselves as more than their bodies as far back as we can trace their thinking about themselves at all. In most human societies, the idea of spirit as different from matter has looked like a natural and even obvious way of describing what we really are. The conviction that people are more than biology is exceedingly persistent.

People who look attentively at their own experience, trying to follow the ancient advice 'Know thyself'', are inclined to identify themselves in overlapping ways as *living bodies, human beings, people, persons, individuals, selves, souls, spirits...* All these ways of beginning to characterize ourselves are apt to lead into scientific, ethical and metaphysical problems. Some of the vocabulary can be kept neutral and value-free. Some of it hardly can, but makes sense only if we are allowed to bring in straight away some concept of *mattering*[10] or even of *transcendence*.

Often people have gone on to find it natural and even obvious to believe that human spirits depend upon a Divine Spirit. When doubts have arisen, they have felt bound to set about finding proofs that God is indeed the explanation of everything. When the proofs look shaky, human longing for some reality beyond this life still comes through only too clearly, and accusations of wishful thinking hit hard.

[9]   See below, Chapter 3.
[10]   See Oppenheimer (1988; 1995/2003).

What we surely know is that there is something wonderful about human existence and about the strange fact that we are conscious subjects as well as objects. Instead of saying, 'Therefore there must be a God to explain it all', it is more promising to say, 'Here are some odd data and here is a complex hypothesis about a Creator God, which has been handed down to us to account for the data. Let us try out this hypothesis and see what happens if we live our lives on this basis.' Some of us find that we can affirm God's reality as the most convincing explanation of human experience. We need to explore together where we can put our faith.

The first disciples of Christ could happily build their creed on the basis of their existing belief in God. For the early Christians, whether they were Jewish or Gentile, more or less learned, more or less devout, it was not as hard as people find it now to recognize realities which go beyond what is simply physical. The founders of our tradition did not have to introduce the Gospel by marshalling arguments against prevalent materialism. They could expect their contemporaries to accept that this world, full of people and things, was made by God who is Spirit. One might commend their simple faith or feel superior to them, but it makes sense to say that beliefs about spirits were part of their terms of reference.

For first century Christians the Holy Spirit, far from being what some theologians used to call 'the forgotten member of the Trinity', was at the centre of their faith. The Spirit was to be found everywhere, manifest rather than controversial, personal, lively, domestic though not domesticated, familiar though not chummy. St Paul was not saying anything incomprehensible when he asserted that 'When we cry "Abba, Father!" it is the Spirit himself bearing witness with our spirit that we are children of God.'[11]

Further reading
Nagel, Thomas (1986) *The view from nowhere.* Oxford University Press.

---

[11]   *Romans* 8.16.

Oppenheimer, Helen (1973) *Incarnation and immanence*. Hodder & Stoughton.

Oppenheimer, Helen (1983) *The hope of happiness*. SCM Press.

Oppenheimer, Helen (1995/2003) 'Mattering, *Studies in Christian ethics*, 8:1 (reprinted in *Approaches to ethics nursing beyond boundaries* ed. Verena Tschudin. Butterworth Heinemann).

Oppenheimer, Helen (2006) *What a piece of work*. Imprint Academic.

Chapter 2

Other People

It is astonishing what foolish things one can temporarily believe if one thinks too long alone.

J.M. Keynes, *The general theory of employment, interest and money*, Preface p. xxiii

As the Christian Church grew among the Gentiles, it was natural for thinking believers to draw upon the resources of Greek philosophy for elucidating their experience. Starting on the basis that human beings are not merely matter which showed signs of life but embodied spirits, they were glad to take up the notion that each person is double, made up of mortal physical flesh and enduring spiritual soul. It was tempting to lose sight of the wholeness of people and proceed to think of the soul as the real person, who is separable from the material body and who is even indestructible. *Dualism* is the theory which is built on this seemingly clear distinctness of body and soul. From this beginning, dualism looked like straightforward Christian orthodoxy. It seemed to be the plainest way to understand the nature of God's human creatures and their hopes and fears.[1]

Though people were evidently made of physical stuff like plants and animals, they could also claim kinship with the angels. Their mortal earthly bodies were somehow attached to heavenly spirits. Sooner or later the soul and the body would be separated by inexorable death, but the promise of resurrection meant that the death of the body need not mean the death of the person. It was the spirit which mattered. No doubt the resurrection of the body was an

---

[1] See Oppenheimer (1988), chapter 3 'Doubleness'.

encouraging idea, established by the rising of Christ, but it was the indestructible soul which guaranteed both our present value and our continuing durability. Dualists could contentedly consign people's bodies to the dust, in the sure and certain hope of a blessed immortality.

Pious people will have no truck with the sceptical materialism which leaves out the soul, which takes the world of physics as all there is and our material bodies as all there is of us. They are naturally inclined to welcome dualism and find it enticingly plausible. They hold on to the twofold character of a human being, happily interpreted for centuries in these terms of a precious immaterial soul which Providence has conjoined with a fleshly body.

Philosophers who follow the dualist tradition find their route straightforward at first. Since thinking is their business, they gladly characterize human beings as thinking creatures, and readily take *soul* to mean much the same as *mind*. The role of minds is to think, while the role of bodies is to keep in touch with things. So each one of us is a conscious mind which experiences the world by way of a responsive body. Though dualists in the tradition of Descartes fall into perplexity about how such different kinds of substance as a mind and a body can actually interact with one another; they have been willing, as part of their faith, to take it for granted that difficulties like this can be overcome, because they have felt sure that dualism must be the Christian view. Perhaps the pineal gland, which seemed to have no particular biological role, might be the place where soul and body were connected?[2]

It is time to state that the difficulties of dualism are not minor complications to be set aside, leaving intact this way of understanding what a person is. The next step is to set up a major problem which dualism can hardly solve. To knock down this Aunt Sally can positively clear the way to a more constructive understanding of what people are.

Sooner or later a dualist needs to ask the question: Since I cannot see into other people's minds, how can I be sure that

---

[2]   'Descartes' in *Oxford companion to the mind* (1987).

these other bodies really do have minds of their own, just as my body does? I cannot seriously doubt that my life among all the people who matter to me is on a secure footing, but has my certainty any firm foundation?[3] This intellectual path, by which persons lose confidence and find themselves separated from one another, is the way to *solipsism*, 'sole-self-ism', the theoretical isolation of the individual mind.

A convinced solipsist would not merely be someone hindered by some kind of insensitivity or disability from communicating with the other people in the neighbourhood. A solipsist would be profoundly alone, for lack of any way of knowing that there were any other people. If this is a real problem it calls for an answer. Our common life depends upon us all being in touch with other people; but how can I as one individual be assured that there really is anyone else to keep me company? Is the 'someone' I am the only one? What justification have I for supposing that there are experiences going on which are not my experiences?

Philosophers in the mid-twentieth century were much exercised by this question, led into it by steps which looked plain. Whether or not they believed in *souls*, they fell into the habit of discussing *selves*, not just 'myself,' 'yourself' and 'themselves', but 'a self' and '*the* self.' 'The self' was to be identified as the conscious mind, in contrast with the physical body. Thinkers therefore had to study 'theory of mind' in order to understand how such a mind and such a body could be properly fastened together to make one person, since they are not just different things but different kinds of thing.

This way of thinking about 'the mind' leads into the kind of dualism which imagines the real self as shut up within a body like a container or even a prison. Each embodied mind is trapped like one lobster in a lobster pot, which is easily entered but whose design prevents its occupant from crawling out again. Solipsism becomes a live threat, in the form of the recalcitrant *problem of other minds*. How does anyone

---

[3] See Oppenheimer (1973), e.g. pp.119–120.

really know that there is anybody else? The intellectual question, how these separated selves can become acquainted with any other selves, had to be of more than intellectual significance. How can individual souls, however valuable each one seems to be, have a lively ethical concern for other individual souls if they can get in touch only indirectly? As John Cook Wilson had said in 1897, 'We don't want merely inferred friends.'[4]

This worry can be answered but some of the proposed answers seemed to separate us from one another more than ever. In an article first published in 1932, H.H. Price[5] started by facing the fact that neither of the current favourite theories would serve. We do not know other people by *analogy* from our knowledge about ourselves. 'They seem like me so they must be like me.' The analogy does not hold. Nor do we know them by direct *intuition* providing a window into other people's minds. 'I just *see* that they are like me.' The intuition is missing. We cannot find one another either by painstaking arguments or by unpropped assertions. 'If I wanted to go to Dublin, I wouldn't be starting from here.'

More promisingly, Price began the process of putting our seemingly fractured common life together again by approaching belief in other people from the opposite direction, not starting from our theoretical worries but from our real experience of being in touch with one another. He did not begin as somebody on the lookout for visiting aliens. He found himself already in a world of language-users, coming across comprehensible symbols which he had not himself originated. This is particularly telling when messages come which give one new information. 'Look out! There's another step!' So communication does work. People do find themselves in touch. Nobody need live alone in the world cut off from everyone else. I do not have to inhabit a lobster pot.

Price thereby laid the foundation for a more constructive understanding of what people are and how they can be related to one another. Instead of treating communication as a desired but difficult objective, which each individual

[4]   Cook Wilson (1926), p. 853; see Oppenheimer (1973), p. 122.
[5]   Price (1932).

must struggle to achieve in order to find anybody else, he recognized the positive communication we already have. He did not make it the *goal* at which we have to aim, but the *basis* of the awareness of one another which we find given. Interaction is where we start, not an uncertain destination we can only hope to reach eventually.

When one considers how fundamental is the given human experience of communicating with one another, it appears that getting in touch is not something people just happen quite often to do. Knowledge of other minds is more than a useful and agreeable addition to what somebody's life could be on its own. Part of the significance of *human being* is a *creature who communicates.*[6] The existence of other people cannot be proved by arguments but it does not need to be, because life together is built all along into the structure of personal existence. The ghost of solipsism can be laid, by understanding that being together is historically and logically prior to being alone.

Price's argument could be strengthened by paying attention to the way human consciousness and self-consciousness arise in practice, that is, by looking at how children do learn who they are and do learn at the same time who other people are. Philosophers may be dubious about this move, because they have been taught that matter-of-fact information about real mothers and babies ought not to be their business. They can be reassured: they are not indulging in anecdotal irrelevant chat, but establishing their terms of reference. To ask about how human lives develop is to engage in the proper philosophical procedure of first identifying the subject matter which is to be considered.

Although the myth of Adam and Eve recounts the creation of humankind as two fully-grown people, in our familiar world every new human being starts as a baby, helpless and ignorant, needing a great deal of help with the task of developing into a person, totally dependent indeed upon the other people whose existence is supposed to be so hard to establish. Babies may be self-centred egoists, but

---

[6]   See Oppenheimer (1988), pp. 54–55, 139.

they really are not solipsists who have to argue their way into human company. There is no trace, either in our own memories or in the way we see children develop, of the momentous event it would have to be to realize for the first time that there is anybody else in the world. How old was I when I first established communication with anybody else? Was it my first smile or my first word which connected me with other people? Instead of suddenly finding Man Friday's footprint on my desert island, I can remember gradual processes of learning, depending from the outset on those other minds for whom philosophers hunt in vain.

'We' is at least as basic as 'I'. 'We need one another to be ourselves,' said John Macmurray, calling this 'the central and crucial fact of personal existence.'[7] 'Relationship', said Chief Rabbi Jonathan Sacks, 'precedes identity.'[8] People who have trouble with understanding this truth have the serious disability which is known as autism.[9]

Indeed there has lately been a good deal of careful study of how what psychologists as well as philosophers call a 'theory of mind' develops from infancy. The question is, 'How does a child become aware that she is like others in having a mind, yet different from others in so far as she has her own feelings, thoughts, beliefs and so on, and other people have theirs?'[10] The answer is confirmed, that 'psychological connectedness' is not a destination but the place from which we set out. Our progress is not from *me* to *you* but from *us* to *you and me*. By sharing human experience all along we come to recognize other people, and we can go on from this beginning to differentiate ourselves from them.[11]

Another way of putting this is to say that a baby's awareness that 'Here is something like me' is a 'primary perceptual judgement'.[12] It is not really a mystery that newborn infants seem to have some sort of innate capacity to take

---

[7]   Macmurray (1961), p. 211.
[8]   Sacks (2004), p. 178.
[9]   See 'Autism' in *Oxford companion to the mind* (1987); Baron-Cohen *et al.* (1993).
[10]   Hobson (1993), p. 209.
[11]   ibid.
[12]   Meltzoff and Gopnik (1993), p. 336.

notice of human faces, even though they have never seen their own faces.[13] Studies of the two-way imitating games mothers play with their babies show that the babies respond particularly, not to any face which happens to be in sight, but to the particular people nearby who make faces at them.[14]

It is easier to learn a lesson than to make a great discovery for oneself. The existence of other minds is not the conclusion of a theoretical argument people work out, but a practical lesson which was taught to each of us about what to expect. The lesson was the reverse of the instruction which the old 'analogical theory' proposed. It was not, 'Here are these other people who look somewhat like you, though so far not very much like you. They really are like you and have inner lives just as you have.' We do believe this but are we being credulous, or even illogical? The lesson we were actually taught, which our experience has constantly confirmed, is 'Here you are and here am I. One day you will grow big and take your place among all of us older people who are looking forward to having you with us.'[15]

It is not belonging but separation which is sophisticated. People are not like gingerbread men stamped out and given their individual identities by being divided from all the other gingerbread men.[16] The ways they belong together and shape one another are more basic than that. The theory which might be called the 'cake-cutter' view of what it means to be *someone* will not do. People's lives consist to a great extent of their dealings with one another. They may understand or misunderstand each other and appreciate or reject other people's company. Whether they prefer to say, like Matthew Arnold on Dover Beach, 'Ah, love, let us be true To one another!' or like Greta Garbo, 'I want to be alone', they do not start alone. To be in a community with other people is the default position for personal life.

---

[13] ibid., p. 355.
[14] ibid.
[15] Oppenheimer (1973), pp. 136–137.
[16] ibid., p. 140.

Somebody with sceptical instincts who still hesitates to make a confident stand here might prefer to move more cautiously. Rather than assuming the right to take the existence of other people for granted, at least it is rational to consider their reality as a working *hypothesis*. The idea that I am one among many and that *we* are sufficiently alike to be inhabitants of one world has worked so well and yielded such fruitful results that it is definitely well established. We can safely live by this conviction and build our moral lives upon it. At least nobody need look on the fact that we have companions as a remarkable though somewhat controversial discovery which most people have somehow succeeded in making.

Faith ought to be glad to abandon the dualist notion of souls which though valuable are elusive souls. Believers are not obliged, any more than unbelievers, to take the person to pieces and then puzzle about how to put the spiritual and the material fragments together again to make one life story. It is not reassuring to think of oneself as a non-physical entity with its own permanence, which is superior to the poor mortal body and readily detachable from it, but only too easily lost when it is detached. The pineal gland is a non-starter. It could never have done the job.

If in due course we start to doubt and argue, and require our original certainty of each other's reality to show its rational credentials, this is where H. H. Price's arguments can come in to call a halt to runaway scepticism. The hypothesis that there are other people, were we tempted to stop granting it, is reasonably confirmed by the fact that all along our efforts to establish communication with one another have positively succeeded.[17] The best proof of the pudding is the eating. Smiling chuckling babies are responding to friendly adults, not sending experimental radio signals across the universe just in case there may be conscious life going on somewhere else.

---

[17]   ibid., pp. 132–133.

The old-fashioned argumentation is not negligible: first, because the problem of other minds is not yet dead.[18] There still persists the tendency for people who are beginning to study philosophy to make it their duty to follow Descartes and doubt whatever they possibly can doubt. Whenever the question is asked. 'How do you know?' they feel obliged to suppose that the matter is uncertain and start looking for proofs.

Secondly and more positively, because Price's answer, which allows the solution to be put in place before the problem has arisen, begins to bring out the fundamental importance of communication with one another as a key to unlock comprehension of what people are. The relationships of individuals are at the root of their real lives. There is no difficult wobbly step out of my own life into a world with other people in it, because I have learned how to say 'me' and 'I' as part of learning how to say 'you' and 'we' and 'it'. Solipsism really can be honourably left behind before it ever takes hold.

Further reading

Oxford companion to the mind (1987), ed. Richard Gregory. Oxford University Press.

Avramides, Anita (2001) *Other minds* in series The problems of philosophy. Routledge.

Buford, Thomas O., ed (1970) *Essays on other minds*. University of Illinois Press and bibliography there.

Baron-Cohen, Simon, Helen Tager-Flusberg & Donald J. Cohen, eds (1993) *Understanding other minds: perspectives from autism*. Oxford Medical Publications.

Macmurray, John (1961) *Persons in relation*. Faber & Faber.

Oppenheimer, Helen (1973) *Incarnation and immanence*. Hodder & Stoughton: Chapters 8 'Oneself and others' and 9 'One world'.

Price, H.H. (1932), 'Our knowledge of other minds', *Proceedings of the Aristotelian Society* Vol. XXXII. See also Buford (1970).

---

[18]   See Avramides (2001); Buford (1970).

Chapter 3

Whole People

And as for the dead being raised, have you not read in the book of Moses, in the passage about the bush, how God said to him, 'I am the God of Abraham, and the God of Isaac, and the God of Jacob?' He is not God of the dead, but of the living.

Mark 12.26–27

It was Gilbert Ryle[1] in the middle of the twentieth century who made the problem of 'knowledge of other minds' old-fashioned, by repudiating the current doctrine of body *plus* mind which had taken people apart to start with. He abandoned the dualist assumption that people are hidden ghosts mysteriously connected with automatic machines, and brought the unity of the person fully back into the philosophical picture. Bodies do not conceal people: on the contrary, they put people, literally, in touch with one another.

Ryle called body/soul dualism a 'category mistake'.[2] Thinking of people's souls as components which can be separated from their bodies is a misunderstanding, rather like walking across someone's lawn, looking at the roses and the shrubs, and asking, 'And now may I see your garden?' If I listen to somebody's entertaining conversation for an hour and complain that I have still not met her soul, that is not a category mistake, but a somewhat pretentious way of saying that I am disappointed by her shallowness, or that she comes across as insincere. It would be a category mistake if I fretted that I never meet the real person however

[1]   Ryle (1949), pp. 16ff.
[2]   ibid., chapter I section 2.

deep our conversation, because somewhere behind her talking, wrinkling her brow and smiling there must be a spirit who is permanently hidden from me.

Likewise Peter Strawson[3] identified the whole person as the primary category. The embodied person is the basic concept which we find given from the start. The traditional components of a human being, spiritual substance and material substance, are real but secondary. Instead of going submissively along with the received view that the real person is a soul who generally has a body but does not particularly need one, Strawson explained the profound awkwardness of this notion of a disembodied spirit.

He pointed out that a being who was quite a different sort of reality from a material object could not interact at all with the physical world which people inhabit and normally take for granted. We should not simply assume that people could lead their lives without their bodies. What could a spirit handle, without hands, or even see, without eyes?[4] Would a spirit hear all, or none, of the noises which are going on in the world? How could a spirit set about connecting its, his, or her own experience with any particular physical happenings? We take it for granted that people are located at particular places and have their own points of view, but we ought to ask what it would mean for a disembodied person to move from one place to another, or indeed to have a specific point of view at all?

People who hope for immortality may wonder how their surviving souls will find other souls and identify one another, without faces, and communicate their thoughts, without throats and lips? Strawson suggested that they would have lonely lives, depending much on their memories. 'No doubt it is for this reason', he remarked, 'that the orthodox have wisely insisted on the resurrection of the

---

[3]   Strawson (1959).
[4]   I discussed this in Oppenheimer (1973), e.g. pp. 26–27.

body.'[5] St Paul would surely have understood what he meant.[6]

Bernard Williams in a review in *Philosophy* suggested that Strawson overstated his case.[7] Perhaps a 'disembodied person could see from a point of view, observe others, think about them ... All that he would lack is bodily contact with others, and being identified by them. He might survive well on such a mental diet.' Logically, that appears reasonable; but morally, to think of such existence as surviving 'well' would seem perversely paradoxical. People who had no means of communication with other people might as well be in solitary confinement. A disembodied spirit would turn out to be fundamentally out of touch, unable to find or recognize any companions, needing to live on memories not on interaction. Christians who believe that they have detachable immortal souls ought to face this problem. They may find themselves glad to set aside dualism and its inaccessible souls with their difficulties of communication.

But it may appear that escaping from the frying pan of solipsism means falling into the fire of scepticism. If bodiless spirits are no better than ineffective ghosts, what happens to people's heavenly hopes? They can see for themselves that bodies are mortal. How can they be assured of life after death, unless the real self is the immortal soul? It is no wonder that believers are attached to the idea that when their bodies die they can rely upon their souls to keep them going, somewhere above the bright blue sky. If in the end their bodies are to be raised incorruptible and each body reunited with its own soul, so much the better.

Christians who are willing to heed the philosophical arguments, rather than brushing them aside, may find their faith illuminated not destroyed. 'Body' and 'soul' are not two kinds of substance interacting with each other like chemicals in a test tube, with predictable or unpredictable

---

[5]   Strawson (1959), pp. 115–116.
[6]   'For in this we groan, earnestly desiring to be clothed upon with our house which is from heaven: If so be that being clothed we shall not be found naked.' *2 Corinthians* 5.2–3.
[7]   Williams (1986).

results. They are two valid ways of referring to the one real life of the same person, living and dying on earth and re-created in heaven.

The life which is now absent from a dead body is not a 'spiritual substance', which has left the material substance and is now somewhere else or nowhere. What has gone, undoubtedly gone, is the characteristic, one might say the power, this body had of being alive. For materialists, once the body is dead that has to be the end of the person, because there is no other kind of substance which can go on living. Dualists cling, with evident difficulty, to two kinds of substance which can be taken apart.

Suppose that one can be a Christian materialist, then the idea can come into its own that there is no need for the soul as a removable item, an entity which may or may not perish when its body dies. It is just as authentic and more comprehensible to think of the soul as the shape, the form, of what matters about a person. 'She has aged a lot in the last few years but she is still the warm-hearted friend she has always been.' 'Her troubles seem to have soured her and I feel we have lost touch.' 'When he said that, I could see him as a small boy again.' Somebody's spirit is a recognizable *pattern*, not unalterable but continuous, which can be identified here and now and which may one day reappear in a different context.[8]

A useful analogy for explaining what religious people mean by 'spirit' is a computer program which may be switched off for a while and switched on again in due course.[9] What makes this analogy so promising is that it allows for a literal continuity between this life and the next which is physically real but does not require the continuity of any material stuff. When the pattern is restored, it is the very same pattern, not merely a substitute.

Philosophers may be intrigued by the question where the data actually are while the program is switched off. Believers meanwhile trust that although this laptop is out-

---

[8] I explored this approach in Oppenheimer (1988); also Oppenheimer (2006), e.g. p. 71.

[9] See Oppenheimer (1988), p. 85.

moded and there are no spare parts to be had any more, the data have been *saved* and will be reliably transferred into new and improved hardware.

The reference to salvation is more than a decorative pun. It is a hint of how a Christian can try to reply to a philosophical difficulty about personal survival which has been called the Replica Objection.[10] If the resurrection of the body means something like the transference of data into another computer, could the pattern of one person be copied more than once and transferred into two or more different resurrection bodies? If that is a good analogy for what resurrection means, could one person be raised from the dead twice? What would we say if twin bodies with twin memories were reborn in the next world, meeting all the criteria for being the same person as somebody who once lived on earth but separate now and developing in different ways? We can make a debating point and reply that this is not going to happen, because there is only one computer expert who holds the copyright. Only God can save the data and restore the pattern; and God can be trusted not to confuse us all by doing this more than once.

The debating point needs to be developed as a significant and essential affirmation about resurrection. To talk sense about what personal identity means, in this world or another, it is not enough to argue about the theory of knowledge and establish logical criteria for counting somebody as the same person in a different time or place. The concept of what it means to be *someone* needs to be enriched with data which belong to ethics. The pattern which constitutes a person is more significant than a bodily shape, or even an abiding collection of memories. What matters is a particular pattern of value: one might say, a pattern of 'lovability'.[11] What makes this analogy so promising is that it allows for a literal continuity between this life and the next which is physically real but does not have to be the continuity of the same material body.

---

[10] See Parfit (1985).
[11] See Oppenheimer (1988), chapter 7.

The point of supposing that God will restore the pattern is the faith that God loves and wants to save this individual, who is not an item in an inventory but a particular precious personality. The Christian hope of survival depends entirely, one might indeed say depends logically, not only on the power of God who is able to save or delete a soul, which a sceptic might point out could be exercised in an arbitrary way, but upon the love of God who cherishes people.

If sceptics are not satisfied with this answer and still wonder whether an extra resurrected person might cause theological chaos by meeting all the criteria for being the same valuable person, they may continue to press the Replica Objection against people's hopes of another life. If a person is essentially a pattern, might the pattern be restored in duplicate or in triplicate? The answer might be 'Well, why not?' The logical point the objection is making might fancifully be allowed. It is conceivable, though it hardly seems likely, that God may want me to have a heavenly twin and may bring to life two people, both going on from where I left off, looking identical at first and having shared the experiences of our earlier life more thoroughly than siblings brought up together. From then on their lives, looks and memories would diverge somewhat or maybe greatly. Philosophers and moralists could occupy themselves in heaven puzzling about intriguing questions, asking which of these twins is their old friend, what self-love means in this context, who is who, and who may be held responsible for what.

When I ask myself, 'If I thought that this was going to happen to me, what would I expect it to be like?' I soon run into difficulties which can make the Replica Objection look stronger than ever. I can tell stories about somebody being duplicated in a future life, much as people tell seemingly coherent stories about time travel between centuries, but the more I go into detail, the less sense the notion makes. Yet once I have started explorations like this it is hard to stop.

The answer a believer can give is that the Replica Objection is really not an objection but a Replica Theory about a possible meaning of resurrection. The hope of heaven can be helpfully expressed as the hope that I shall be replicated by God. If I am raised from death, philosophers can say, if they like, that I am what they mean by a Replica. The awkward idea that then there would be nothing to stop God from creating several copies of me need not constitute a logical or moral objection to Christian faith, any more than the idea that there would be nothing to stop God from raising up baboons instead of people. There is no reason to be concerned about any such prospect.

Without God, there are no replicas to puzzle us. With God, the resurrection of a person is no arbitrary happening which might get out of hand, but, precisely, an 'act of God'. Therefore it is not cheating for a Christian believer to say, 'God knows best.' What would stop God from creating multiple copies of me would be God's decision that this should not be done. If there is another life at all, it will make sense. It would be surprising to encounter two people leading their separate heavenly lives with their conjoined memories, but they could both be well assured that their complex biographies must be a fulfilment of God's purposes. To give scope to such fancies for lighting up theological enquiry is not irreverent, but it would be presumptuously irreverent to present fancies as arguments and conclude them with a confident Q.E.D.

Less fantastic though still mind-stretching, the notion that God will raise people up in another world need not be written off as hopelessly naive. On the contrary, the idea of heaven as a real material place somewhere else, with its own physical laws, looks compatible with some of the baffling notions about multi-dimensional universes which seem to be comprehensible to physicists. 'How I wish', said Austin Farrer, 'we could explain the Einsteinian theory to St Augustine!'[12]

It is strange that Christians, of all people, have welcomed assurances that human beings have immortal souls, as if that were the most reliable basis for their eternal hope. The

---

[12] Farrer (1964), p. 145.

Christian faith is not that persons are bound to survive by their own nature. People who have heavenly hopes have agreed too readily that it is quite all right for their mortal bodies to perish, because they can be sure that their inde-structible souls will persist anyway.

The ordinary human experience of living and ageing is not much like being a vigorous soul who is always in the prime of life, who at present is inconveniently trapped in an increasingly feeble body, but who can hope one day to be set free. It is a matter of being one particular person, whose energy both physical and mental will be used up by the eve-ning. At the end of the day, and analogously at the end of their lives, people fall asleep sooner or later, but they believe that tomorrow they will wake up refreshed, woken by their alarm clocks or by the Last Trump. The resurrection hope is that the recognizable worthwhile pattern of a whole human being, bodily and spiritual, will be re-created after death and given new life by the power of God the Creator. The saved data, for which so much trouble has been taken, are not going to be lost.

As theologians feel at home with 'the soul', so philoso-phers feel at home with 'the self'. They ought likewise to realise that nobody's continued existence depends upon the importance and value of a distinct entity which can be iden-tified as a 'self'. My *self* is a sophisticated notion which can be useful if I take up analytical thinking about the subject called 'theory of mind'. It is not the way I naturally think about the person I find myself to be all along or about the other people I meet all the time.

Christians have too easily lost sight of the ordinary commonsense notion that each of us is an embodied person who lives in a physical environment in touch with many others. It is the people we meet every day, not ghosts who have taken up residence in machines, who make up our human world. I can abandon the idea of a special hidden mind, soul or self which is really 'me', somehow enclosed within a material body which shuts me into my own experi-ence and separates me from everybody else.

I need not give up soul-language, which still provides a convenient and by no means obsolete vocabulary for calling attention to the spiritual meaning of human life. We need this language and can use it without talking nonsense; but it always needs to be applied to complete people, who can identify one another even in remarkably changed circumstances and recognize one another's permanent value.

Though the dualist idea of the surviving soul which developed from Greek philosophy seemed plain to thinking Christians from early days,[13] it really need not be an essential part of the Christian faith. The Gospel has more complex roots in the natural world. The Christian understanding of the meaning of 'spirit' and the nature of human souls and human bodies is firmly grounded in ancient Hebrew ideas of what human creatures are, less sophisticated than dualism maybe, but more down-to earth. .

Spirit, in the Hebrew language, has the straightforward meaning of *breath*. In the creation story in the first chapter of the book of Genesis, the Spirit of God is breathed into Adam and brings him to life, in*spir*ing him in a more physical and literal way than we think of inspiration now. Some Christian theologians, including the present writer, have been glad to seize upon the biblical emphasis on whole bodily persons and deplore the Greek partiality for other-worldly souls.[14] 'Resurrection not immortality' has been a favourite slogan for upholding the hope for human life after death.

Professor James Barr has shown that Hebrew notions about the human person were more complicated than these simple alternatives and that the sharp contrast between Hebrew *holism*, affirming whole people, and Greek *dualism*, affirming souls and bodies, is not so clear.[15]A Christian who is no biblical expert may be grateful for his more subtle elucidation, without being entirely overcome by his cheerful demolition work. It is still promising, indeed it is still crucial, for Christians to keep emphasizing the wholeness of human creatures, body and spirit as one person, even if that

---

[13] See above, p. 11.
[14] See Cullmann (1958).
[15] See Barr (1992).

emphasis cannot be claimed as an especially characteristic part of our Jewish heritage.

The resurrection of the body cannot be merely an optional extra for Christians. If their hope of eternal life could really be grounded upon natural immortality, believers ought to take it for granted that bodily dying is not important. However kindly they are told that the beloved person they are mourning has only slipped away into the next room, they do not find it easy to have such confidence that death is trivial; and nor should they. The courage of martyrs and the consolation of bereaved people do not depend on being able to think, 'Never mind. It really doesn't matter. People's souls cannot die. They simply travel to a better place.' Christians have not been taught to deny that death is fearful. The Lord went to the Cross by way of Gethsemane.[16] The God Christians have been taught to trust has overcome death and has the power to restore dead people to life.

Professor Barr indeed expressed this very conviction in a different way. The conclusion of his book was that the lively hope of immortality is indeed not a human birthright but a divine gift. He took hold of the promise contained in the ancient myth of the tree of life. Adam and Eve were forbidden to eat the fruit. 'Humanity was not fit to come near the tree. Nevertheless the tree remained there in the garden. Later one came to redeem the defect of humanity. Immortality was brought to light.'[17] This way of using the terminology of immortality is not an offer of ghostly survival but of replenished life.

The Christian hope of eternal life depends on being raised by God. The slogan 'resurrection not immortality' tries to capture the essential point that human spirits have no built-in permanence of their own. Christians know this well. When they are gratefully praising God's grace, they are thoroughly aware of their entire dependence. It is when they are theorizing about what it means to be a person that they sometimes get carried away by the idea that what

---

[16] *Matthew* 26.36–46 / *Mark* 14.32–42.
[17] Barr (1992), p. 116.

guarantees someone's survival is that person's own immortal soul.

Further reading

Barr, James (1992) *The garden of Eden and the hope of immortality*. SCM Press.

Cullmann, Oscar (1958) *Immortality of the soul or resurrection of the dead?* Epworth Press.

Oppenheimer, Helen (1973) *Incarnation and immanence*. Hodder & Stoughton: Chapter 2 'Persons and bodies'.

Oppenheimer, Helen (1988) *Looking before and after* (The Archbishop of Canterbury's Lent Book). Collins Fount.

Oppenheimer, Helen (1990) 'Spirit and body', *Theology* March/April.

Oppenheimer, Helen (1995/2003) 'Mattering, *Studies in Christian ethics*, 8:1 (reprinted in *Approaches to ethics nursing beyond boundaries* ed. Verena Tschudin. Butterworth Heinemann).

Oppenheimer, Helen (2006) *What a piece of work*. Imprint Academic.

Ryle, Gilbert (1949) *The concept of mind*. Hutchinson.

Strawson, Peter (1959) *Individuals*. Methuen.

Chapter 4

The Persistent Notion of Spirit

There may be intelligences or sparks of the divinity in millions — but they are not Souls until they acquire identities, till each one is personally itself ... How then are souls to be made? How then are these sparks which are God to have identity given them — so as ever to possess a bliss peculiar to each one's individual existence? How, but by the medium of a world like this?

John Keats, *Letter to George and Georgiana Keats*
April 1819

While philosophers, including Christians, were occupied with dualist theories which separated a person into a body and a soul, scientists, including Christians, were studying the whole physical creation. The Christian creeds affirm that there is one God who is Maker of heaven and earth. Far from impeding the practice of science, the conviction that the universe has a Creator is a positive encouragement to believers with enquiring minds to serve God by studying God's works.

But the course of true love between faith and reason has not run smooth. Faithful as the scientists might want to be, the more successfully they described and explained the material universe, the less they seemed to need any idea of spiritual reality after all. Scholarly orthodoxy ceased to feel bound to recognize 'soul' as a significant category. The terminology of spirit seemed obsolete and the questions this language raised about what persons really are no longer wanted answers.

By the mid-twentieth century, people who valued the name of 'modern' were welcoming the idea that it was time to clear away metaphysics so that physics could be the whole story. The affirmation of anything spiritual, beyond the material things which could be seen, touched and measured, looked like naive superstition or obstinate dogma. Immortal souls could be phased out. Instead of dualism, rational materialism could be installed as the default position. It might still be quite convenient in some practical contexts to differentiate matter and mind, body and soul; but even when this language was used it came to seem natural and straightforward to select *matter* and *body* as fundamental, whereas *mind* was puzzling and *soul* was dubious. If the meaning of life thereupon faded, humanity must be daring enough to come of age, put away childish things and stop believing in fairy stories.

But in the meanwhile the picture has been changing again and materialism has loosened its grip. While public opinion has been learning to be more scientific, physics itself has come to look more metaphysical. Whether 'souls' come into the picture or not, the nature of the everyday world of material bodies has turned out not to be lucid and graspable.

> Nature, and Nature's laws lay hid in night.
> God said, *Let Newton be!* and all was light.
> It did not last: the Devil howling 'Ho!
> Let Einstein be!' restored the status quo.[1]

Physicists, like theologians, have to be ready to hold on to unimaginable and seemingly incompatible concepts if they take their data seriously. The beautiful equations which are the tools of their trade cannot be translated into common-sense language. Since nature itself confronts human beings with mystery which appears not merely puzzling but awesome, thinking people need not feel obliged to banish faith as an alien intruder. When the discoverable nature of the physical world is found to be profoundly paradoxical, believers may be allowed some paradoxes of their own. While scientists struggle with the conflicting characteristics

---

[1]   Squire (1926), adapting Pope's Epitaph for Sir Isaac Newton 1730.

of waves and particles, theologians are not unreasonable to keep struggling with the doctrine of the Trinity who is both three and one.

Down-to-earth scientists need not routinely relegate the idea of spirit to an inaccessible unearthly realm which they can proceed to ignore as imaginary. They may still responsibly believe that the material world which they are studying owes its existence to God who is Spirit. They will have to try to explain why they think this is true, but they are not talking evident nonsense when they go on telling the story of creation. The ancient vivid myth of a supernatural Artisan who shaped creatures by hand out of clay is still usable; but believers who have become too sophisticated to be comfortable with the picture-language need not be stuck in this way of expressing their faith. They may welcome a more austere image of God the Creator as a supreme mathematician, the Inventor of this strange universe beyond straightforward human understanding.

Piety is not obliged to resist the account of reality given by physics. There is no need for believers to keep searching for convenient flaws in the scientific description of the material world, which might with luck let an emaciated 'God of the gaps' push through the holes, like a dog through a cat-flap, when scientific explanation is at a loss. God the Creator owns and inhabits the whole strange universe all along.

Scientists on the other hand are not obliged to resist religious belief and take sceptical materialism as their default position. There is no need for them routinely to delete mystery, nor to treat spiritual reality as an optional attachment, as if that were an advance in understanding. Though they appropriately omit everything but bare material facts from their particular accounts of work in progress, they need not claim to be including everything there really is. The mysterious immensity and intricacy of the natural world undermine the mind-set which banishes all but physical data from a true account of the universe.

Distinguished scientist-theologians have explored these possibilities and earned the attention of thinking people.[2]

Believers and unbelievers may agree that there can be realities which go beyond physics and chemistry. Whether there is a God or not, scholarly honesty can allow space in the whole scheme of things for true statements about transcendence, recognizing both awe-inspiring beauty and moral goodness. The universe is not value-free. People who study its contents should not let the physical sciences relentlessly colonize the whole of human experience.

It is promising to work on the basis that values are not merely added on to reality by human imagination but are really *there*, independently of people's choosing. Commonsense should be brave enough to withstand the dismissiveness of philosophers. It is a reasonable conviction that real objective 'mattering' is strong enough to stand its ground. Ethics cannot and need not be cast out of the world of facts and exiled to some sort of fairyland which we have to devise for ourselves. It may not always be a 'category mistake'[3] to allow 'good' and 'ought' to be built into everyday 'is'. Facts, after all, seldom present themselves to people as 'value-free' and it is difficult to treat them as if they were.

To look at the familiar but marvellous phenomenon of conscious awareness as especially 'value-laden' should be an encouraging habit. 'There is someone here' is a statement which carries more significance than 'This object is solid'. The remarkable fact that conscious experience is such an ordinary occurrence in the natural world is itself a value-laden reality which deserves recognition.

There is more to people than their outward appearance: they do have inner lives and their inner lives matter. What Mary Midgley has called the 'behaviourist frost' is 'beginning to thaw.'[4] Consciousness can properly be readmitted into factual descriptions of the natural world. Moralists may be glad to recognize that personal life is where values

---

[2]   Such as Ian Barbour, Arthur Peacocke, John Polkinghorne; see e.g. Polkinghorne (2001).

[3]   See above, p. 20.

[4]   Midgley (2006), p. 212.

have a foothold in reality. It is people's consciousness of being themselves, alive among other people, which inserts mattering into the world by bringing in minding.[5] Persons, as they come to know one another, are where 'is' lets in 'ought.'

Suppose next, as most human beings have always supposed: that beyond the real goodness and loveliness people recognize in their experience of the world they inhabit together, something more again is needed for an account of what human beings are. This is where people who find themselves aware of something *more* begin to talk about spiritual meaning. Beyond morality and beauty, people find holiness. Beyond approval and enjoyment, there is reverence. Beyond ethics, wonder makes way for worship.

Talking about realities going beyond ordinary experience is difficult for human beings, because as fallen creatures we are apt to damage what we try to handle. When words are bandied about without due care and attention, 'transcendent' is obscurely technical, 'beautiful' sounds pretentious, 'worthy' is stodgy, 'pious' is prim, 'mystical' belongs to the vocabulary of an in-group, 'sublime' suggests affectation and 'soulful' has an almost unpleasant character. The effort still has to be made to find ways of expressing the experienced realities which these ways of speaking try to capture.

The notion of the sacred has been spelt out in practice in the specific language of religious traditions. People do not generally begin with a broad theory of what 'supernatural' might mean and then consider how to apply it to human life. They begin by considering their own experience and sometimes find the idea of sacredness included in it. In our tradition, Jewish and then Christian believers encountered holiness through the history of people who found themselves chosen by God. The piety of the children of Israel was validated in their experience, in something like the way that the love of husbands and wives is validated in their married life. This confidence is not an irresponsible fantasy: something substantial is going on, even if words for capturing it

---

[5]   See above, p. 8; also Oppenheimer (1983; 1995/2003).

are lacking. Christians today can establish themselves gratefully in the history of God's people and identify themselves as a continuing part of it.

Believers are naturally tempted to be possessive of their own understanding of holiness. They feel sure that even though they may share moral goodness with sceptics, the heights and depths of life must belong specially to them. Rather than being jealously determined to claim a monopoly of spiritual meaning, they might be generous as well as loyal by taking to heart the Gospel saying, 'He that is not against us is for us.'[6] Assured as Christians are, that *their* Lord is the Way, the Truth and the Life, on whom all hope for human beings depends, they are not thereby authorized to restrict his grace to the proper channels. There could be other routes to his kingdom than theirs. At least they could bear in mind the promising maxim that the longest way round may sometimes be the shortest way home.

Many thinking people today, too cautious to pursue holiness by climbing the old and sometimes wobbly ladder of established doctrine, are still hoping to reach the proposed destination. They are trying to scramble up by other routes to the region of the sacred and are equipping themselves for their journey with the concept of 'spirit'. They may not find precise theology a help, but they are in no hurry to shed uplifting religion. Mary Midgley commented that the 'long banished' notion of the spiritual 'seems lately to have been paroled and returned to circulation in a favourable sense.'[7] People who are leaving aside conventional religious commitment are not necessarily subsiding into materialism. The battle of faith and scepticism looks less ferocious but more confusing now than it used to be.

When people refrain from theology but keep on using the concept of the 'spiritual', in order to include in their understanding of what it means to be a person something *more*, something *higher* or *deeper*, than mere matter, this is far from 'secularization'. They are embarking upon a 'broad search

---

[6]   *Mark* 9.40 / *Luke* 9.50.
[7]   Midgley (2006), p. 223.

for meaning, purpose and hope.'[8] There may be no hostility here to orthodoxy, even though orthodoxy is sidetracked. If what truly matters in life is approachable in this way, the people who share the conviction that materialism is not enough can co-operate positively over many of their concerns, not least the education of their children.

Children ought not to be either obstinately indoctrinated, or just as fanatically deprived of their religious heritage. Nor need their immaturity be patronized.[9] Rather than telling them a few selected suitable Bible stories as the whole substance of their spiritual instruction, creative teachers find ways of branching out and encouraging their pupils to use their imaginations more freely, to look for the kinds of meaning which are to be found in their own and other people's everyday experience and to live by these. Watering a plant is a more spiritual exercise than drawing maps of St Paul's missionary journeys.

A criticism Christian believers can still fairly make of these alternative quests is vagueness. Fashionable spirituality is not to be written off as impious, but it must be said that often it is woolly. Prosaic caution has the right, indeed the duty, to keep enquiring: Does this mean anything? Is it honest? How are we to find out whether this way of looking really is the best way to understand human life, or no more than a flight of fancy? What criteria are we supposed to apply? Still more urgently, can the lofty notion of spiritual meaning reckon with the fact that in the end people are mortal and all of them are faced by death, however significant and valuable their lives are in the meantime? Because truth matters as well as kindness, to keep pressing such severe enquiries is not to be hastily condemned as cruel.

Mid-twentieth century logical positivists, who insisted that statements which claim to mean anything must have definite application to findable facts, were raising questions which always need to be faced. Their philosophy looks old-fashioned now and metaphysics can be respectable

---

[8] Woodward (2008), p. 49.
[9] I discussed Christian theology, as it might make sense to children, in Oppenheimer (1994).

again, but the positivist message still deserves attention. Whether a statement makes enough sense to be true or false has something to do with how we can find out whether it is true or not. Does metaphysical language about spiritual reality even say anything, let alone tell the truth, unless it is open to being falsified by what happens? To understand people's speech, we do not need to know whether they are speaking the truth, but we do need to have some idea what difference it would make for their statements to be either true or false. It remains reasonable to stipulate that uplifting assertions, if they are supposed to say anything significant, must be open to being confirmed or refuted. When Owen Glendower boasted that he could 'call spirits from the vasty deep', Hotspur retorted,

> Why, so can I, or so can any man;
> But will they come when you do call for them?[10]

Particularly, but not only, when faith affirms that there is *Someone* there, there is more at stake than a general intention to look hopefully upon human life whatever happens. Valid hopes need to be based upon some particular truth: indeed, to put it bluntly, on some kind of objective fact making a difference to the actual world. Faith can be as decisively lost by being watered down and explained away, the 'death by a thousand qualifications,'[11] as it can be lost by being logically disproved.

Christian possessiveness about whatever truth, beauty and goodness people can find and share is still not in order. The sea of faith which Matthew Arnold heard withdrawing, like the ebbing tide retreating over the pebbles on Dover Beach, left behind it some solid meaning in life which could still be grasped and held:

> Ah, love, let us be true
> To one another!

To believe in other human beings is to adhere to values by making a stand on facts. To say 'I trust you' may be sound or it may be silly but it is not dubiously metaphysical. We

---

[10]　*King Henry IV, Part I*, III. i. 52–54.
[11]　See Flew (1955), p. 97.

understand what circumstances make such a declaration appropriate. People can reliably make life worth living for one another. Suppose they find that the metaphorical tide of faith comes in again, as literal tides do, they will not have turned away from belief in a trustworthy God by being true to one another in the meantime. They may have done something to rehearse for it.

Further reading

Flew, Anthony (1955) 'Theology and falsification' in *New essays in philosophical theology*, ed. Flew and MacIntyre. SCM Press.

Midgley, Mary (2006) 'On Dover Beach' *Philosophy*, April.

Oppenheimer, Helen (1994) *Finding & following*. SCM Press.

Polkinghorne, John, ed. (2001) *The work of love: creation as kenosis*. SPCK.

Chapter 5

People and Values

Your enjoyment is never right, till you esteem evry Soul so great a Treasure as our Savior doth.

Thomas Traherne, *Centuries*, I. 39

Many people, whether they are believers or unbelievers, find meaning in their lives through their relationships with their fellow creatures. Looking at the significance of 'human being' is a straightforward starting-place for enquiring about what gives meaning to life, because we can, literally, look at human beings and know what we mean to consider. We can recognize that whatever turns out to matter, at any rate human beings matter. They evidently provide the most promising examples of value identifiable in everyday life, whether one believes that human beings are first of all children of God, or whether one thinks that they are on their own in the universe.

Anyone who regards human beings as worthwhile may claim, with care, the honourable name of *humanist*.[1] The concept of 'humanism' has confusingly gone through some changes of meaning. It would be pedantic to try to restore to ordinary use its original particular connotation of Renaissance classical learning. It is still not compulsory to accept the present prevailing usage, in which 'humanism' has been requisitioned for affirming human value without God. This negative meaning may be quite difficult to uproot, but the effort to weed out smothering sceptical assumptions is worth making, in order to clear the common ground on which we could all stand.

[1]   Oppenheimer (2006), pp. 26f.

Believers and unbelievers together should be able to start with a more positive humanism, insisting that human beings really do matter 'to whom it may concern', whether there is or whether there is not any deity to be concerned for them. Christians and friendly sceptics ought to be able to realize a promising initial cooperation, without forcing an instant confrontation between faith and doubt. Religious people may join with sceptics in paying grateful attention to the special value which they can find in one another and in themselves. Respect for other people does not require self-abasement, but on the contrary should encourage positive unpretentious self-respect.

On this basis it is not strange nor illogical for humanists to be Christians, and likewise it is not strange nor illogical for Christians to be humanists. Christian humanists are not sinking themselves disloyally in the world's values. Affirming that human beings matter is a step towards the awe-inspiring affirmation that they matter to God their Maker.

So it is fitting for Christians to celebrate the glory of human beings, not, of course, as their own achievement but as derived from the glory of the Creator: 'and behold, it was very good'.[2] In spite of the manifest prevalence of human pride, it would be a shame for Christians to be ungrateful for the marvel of humankind, as if they were determined to notice only human weakness and badness. The delight Christians take in creaturely value may sound more suitably pious if they desist from putting the emphasis on the dangerous glory of outstanding individuals. Basing their gratitude more securely on the conviction that human souls are all sacred, they can celebrate the wonder and the spiritual significance of humanity.

One way to give humanism a bad name is to magnify humanity by ignoring or belittling the whole animal kingdom to which we belong. It is high time to outgrow the habit of mind which has distinguished *men* insensitively from the

---

[2]   *Genesis* 1.31.

beasts who are our ancestors and cousins.[3] Proper celebration of humanity will refuse to separate human beings from
their context in the natural world. 'We are earthly creatures
who are thoroughly *at home* here — part of the system, native
to the planet' insisted Mary Midgley in an article in *Philosophy*.[4]

Christians ought to have been enthralled to learn from
Darwin how wonderfully interconnected the world of biology is. They could have been inspired to contemplate the
grandeur and patience of the Creator who set all this in
motion. Indeed some of them are so inspired, but too many
have been inclined to take fright. Some people are still taking refuge in denial that evolution happened at all.

Others, more plausibly, have swung the other way,
accepting evolution and rejecting the ancient assumption
that humanity is the crown of creation.[5] No longer will they
arrogantly elevate human beings as the rational animals.
Instead they may come to despise human beings as naked
apes with very little to commend us. Alongside or even
above human rights they set animal rights. The ferocity of
some upholders of the status of animals is an unhappy but
not surprising reaction to the long-standing complacent
assumption of human dominance: just as the strident
aggressiveness of some feminists has followed unhappily
but naturally upon generations of repression by complacent
men.

Believers and unbelievers alike ought to consider the
urgency and complexity of moral arguments about other
creatures and the ways human beings treat them, but they
cannot give priority to every question at once. To start with
humankind as a given fact is still a firm basis for ethical
thinking. The related notions which attach themselves to
the familiar concept of a human being, notions such as
person, individual, soul, spirit,[6] represent connected but not
identical ideas whose significance needs disentangling.

---

[3]   See Oppenheimer (2006).
[4]   See Midgley (2006).
[5]   See above, p. 1; also Oppenheimer (2006), chapters 1 and 4.
[6]   See above, p. 8.

From the overlapping ways in which thinking Christians and sceptics identify the creatures they are, they can hope to discover and develop the values which emerge from these variegated notions.

The category of *person* overlaps with the category of *human being* without exactly coinciding with it. It is indeed a live question whether some non-human animals should be counted as persons. It looks as if early human embryos are not yet persons. If there are angels, or if there were extraterrestrial visitors, they would be persons but not human beings. To be a personal*ist* is to make a stand about the moral significance of persons, a stand which is akin to humanism but not quite interchangeable with it.

'Personalism' may sound less humane than 'humanism'; but the impression it may give of arid technicality could be unfair. No doubt when people identify themselves as personalists it is generally with the idea of attending to philosophical problems, but these studies can hardly be severely academic, or 'personal' would mean '*im*personal'. Enquiry about what it means to be a person, and what ethical consequences follow, leads straight into questions which are just as humanly interesting and practically illuminating as enquiry about the nature and value of the human beings among whom we live. The plural of 'a person' is not always desiccated formal 'persons'. It is everyday *people* whom we meet and get to know.

Whereas we talk about *human beings* when we want to compare and contrast them with other living creatures, the point of using the terminology of *persons* is generally to contrast them with *things*. A person is primarily and essentially an *I*: a *who* not a *what*, a conscious subject, not an inert object. A thing is a body located at a particular place. A person is located at a place and conscious of being so. The fundamental difference, the difference which matters, between a person and a thing is that a person has a point of view.[7] A person has a perspective, a viewpoint, from which to experience the world and to become active in the world.

---

[7]   See above, pp. 3, 21.

One might go so far as to define a person as a living point of view.[8]

Does it therefore follow that some animals, who surely have points of view and ought not to be treated as things, really do qualify as persons? Not many people believe that shellfish are persons and some vegetarians are prepared to eat them, but people are often inclined to think that chimpanzees and dogs are persons, and perhaps many other fellow-creatures including dolphins. Tom Regan posed the question constructively by asking whether a creature is 'the subject of a life'.[9] Jeremy Bentham spoke up for compassionate utilitarianism when he insisted eloquently that what made a creature's point of view morally significant was not whether that creature could *think* but whether it could *suffer*.[10]

Just as the concept of 'human being' overlaps with the concept of 'person', so in turn 'person' is an approximate synonym for 'individual'. It was Boethius in the sixth century, in prison facing his own death with the support of philosophy, who provided the traditional definition of a person as 'the *individual* substance of a *rational* nature.'[11] This formula belongs to a history in which it seemed natural for people who were looking for self-understanding to put all the emphasis upon their wonderful gift of reason, at the expense of many other characteristics which also make us human. The prominence Boethius gave to rationality seems incomplete and even misleading today, but it is still worth building on his affirmation that understanding the meaning of 'person' is connected with understanding the meaning of 'individual'.

An individual is a being that can be singled out and identified again. Individuals receive names.[12] While human*ism* emphasizes the excellence of human beings as creatures in the natural world, and personal*ism* emphasizes the moral significance of conscious life, 'individual' too has its 'ism'.

[8]   See Oppenheimer (1988), pp. 67f.
[9]   Regan (2004).
[10]   Bentham (1789), chapter 17.
[11]   *De consolatione philosophiae* c. AD 524.
[12]   Chapter 10, below; see Oppenheimer (2006), chapter 7 'Recognizing'.

What individualism emphasizes is the special significance of every particular self. People are not interchangeable. To identify them by numbers rather than names is to do them wrong. People are not units in a heap nor even flock animals in a herd, bundled tidily or cosily together but still fundamentally replaceable. Individuals matter separately and each one is 'I'.

Whether 'human being', 'person' or 'individual' is taken as the key, each of these connected concepts stands for a kind of being which matters. This means that the difference between 'something' and 'someone' is an *ethical* difference. It is morally and maybe logically impossible to be entirely neutral about human beings, persons, individuals, in the way we can be neutral about things. 'I care for nobody, no not I' is an inhuman aberration. People make moral demands which ought to be heeded, whereas we are allowed to look on things indifferently without minding whether they come or go. 'There is someone there' is a statement which does more than assert a fact: it has implications about appropriate reactions. Here is a place where the notorious gap between stating the facts and making moral judgments is narrow, a place which provides an ideal site for building a bridge from *is* to *ought*.

Twentieth-century philosophers perceived the gap as huge. Facts and values belonged in different worlds. People who tried to jump straight across from what is true to what ought to be done were liable to fall into a dangerous chasm. They shied away from the edge and tried to mark off a definite boundary between the two realms; because they had learnt thoroughly, even too thoroughly, from David Hume that it was a logical mistake to ignore the gap and to try to reach 'ought' from 'is'.[13] The fact that 'She *is* my baby' could not establish that 'I *ought* to look after her' unless these statements were properly attached by the moral imperative, 'Look after your baby!'[14]

---

[13] Hume (1740).
[14] R.M. Hare was the distinguished exponent of this way of understanding the nature of ethics, e.g. Hare (1952)

Moral philosophers were taught by G. E. Moore to call the direct move from *is* to *ought* the 'naturalistic fallacy.'[15] They were convinced that to commit this was an elementary error. So indeed it can be. 'They are asking for money' does not immediately imply 'You ought to give them some'. 'He is all-powerful' does not entail, 'You ought to worship him.' Yet there are bridges in many places across the is-ought gap which make it crossable after all.[16] In the twenty-first century it seems possible to relate the two worlds of fact and value in ways which might have shocked the philosophy teachers of one's youth. 'If we put enough "ought" into the "is" to start with, it will be there ready for us to get out again when we need it.'[17]

Not all facts are value-free, especially not facts about people. Thinking rightly about reality is not always a matter of first making morally neutral statements and then trying, as a separate exercise, to stick on the values, hoping that the join will hold. The statement 'Here *is* someone in pain' does not need special ethical glue to fix it on to 'I *ought* to do something to help'. What people need, in order to live as moral agents, is to be aware of accessible values which are not in a world apart, separate from the facts of the case, but *built in* to the facts. Instead of saying disapprovingly that a judgment is 'value-loaded' when it ought to be neutral, we should keep on insisting that everyday reality is often not neutral but 'value-laden'.[18]

We may think of things as well as people as making moral claims; but things cannot value themselves. Some particular thing may have a meaning which makes it matter what happens to it, but if so that meaning has been given to it by someone. 'This was the first present she gave me.' 'That is a superb example of his early style.' 'The marks on that rock are stone age drawings.' 'We have four tickets for the opera.' 'An old pound coin is worth as much as a new-

---

[15]   Moore (1929).
[16]   See Emmet (1966) for the idea of a 'bridge notion'. See Oppenheimer (1975), pp. 10–11.
[17]   Oppenheimer (1975), p. 10.
[18]   ibid. p. 11; see also above, p. 34.

minted one.' 'A Roman denarius was once a day's wage, but so many have been dug up that our local museum will not want it.' When things are precious, it is because people set value on them or find value in them: 'And then my heart with pleasure fills And dances with the daffodils.'[19] 'Don't throw that away: somebody might be glad of it'. To say that something has no value is to say that it does not matter to anyone, that nobody minds about it.

People are the primary example of what it means to be 'value-laden'. Thinking about the meaning of life means thinking about people's lives as having built-in value. There is more to a person than bare facts with no moral implications. The concept 'person' includes 'ought' as well as 'is'. Far from committing a fallacy, these statements identify the place where the idea of 'spiritual' reality is able to find a foothold in the world we know. To say that people have built-in value is one way of asserting that they have souls, or rather that they are souls.

The move from the terminology of *human beings, persons,* and *individuals,* which are recognizable as visible and tangible, to the terminology of *souls* and *spirits,* which are recognizable as valuable, can be made without confusing what is with what ought to be.[20] To understand what persons are, we need to use language which does not exclude ethics from the world of facts but plants values firmly in the everyday life of human beings.

A main advantage of approaching the meaning of personal life from this direction, with the value of people securely placed in its earthly context, is that this way of comprehending human beings does not need puzzling extra items called souls to preserve people's value for them. The high-minded dualism which takes spirit and body apart is by-passed. Thinking people have been needlessly enticed to disembody the soul, to disparage the body, to belittle the animals with whom we have so much in common and to suppose that it takes an immaterial spirit to be a carrier of value.

[19] William Wordsworth, 'Daffodils'.
[20] Oppenheimer (1975), p. 11; also see above, p. 34.

There is no realistic role for souls as detachable entities.[21] Belief in the human spirit does not depend upon the viability of a ghost belonging to another world than this, mysteriously connected with a material body which is a thing in the physical world. Instead, the 'soul' is an idea we can comprehend and use, provided we take it to indicate the whole person, considered as morally important.

To affirm the wholeness of bodily persons living in a physical world[22] which itself can be called 'very good' is to give ourselves permission to be less vague and more matter-of-fact about spiritual reality. Soul-language is one way of making room in the universe for the key notion of mattering,[23] which adds a graspable third dimension to the flat bare world of plain scientific fact. Values, so to say, demand recognition because they stick out and cast shadows. We can be ready to consider value as a sort of reality, after all, and acknowledge it wherever we find it, especially in living conscious people.

The upshot of the argument so far is that the primary bearers of value are the people we meet.[24] We keep in contact with values by keeping in contact with people, literally as well as metaphorically. We meet them, we hear, see and touch them, and we find that they do indeed matter. A person is a gateway letting value into the world of physical reality, a place where *what is* can have a rendezvous with *what ought to be*, even if philosophers try to keep them apart.

It is a fact about people that they mind about what happens to them and mind about other people. Their minding is part of their reality and brings into being all manner of definite and complex moral obligations. The duties people owe to one another belong to the real world. Just as what I should believe is something given, although I may not always find it easy to discover, so what I should do is something given, although I may find it hard to discern. Moral obligations are more like matters of fact, which have to be

[21]   See above, pp. 20–21, 23.
[22]   See above, pp. 27–28.
[23]   See Oppenheimer (1995/2003).
[24]   See above, pp. 24, 34.

recognized, than they are like optional ideals which people can choose to adopt or reject. I cannot settle for myself what shall be right by nominating my own values among assorted moral alternatives, any more than I can settle for myself what shall be real by making a free choice among the material data on offer.

The way the argument goes on from here is not as obvious as it might seem. Once I have said that people's minding matters, and therefore that other people lay real moral claims upon me, am I to go straight on to say that human persons have absolute value? When the question is asked, 'Is human life sacred?' many people are glad to reply Yes, but not so many are able to agree about what follows from that. Before ideas about the 'sanctity of human life' can be put into practice, there is ambiguity to sort out concerning what this sacredness of people means. Evidently it must mean that human beings really matter, but one can assert that without making such a big claim as saying that human value is 'absolute'. Human life might be valuable, even sacred, without being *all* that matters and without being unquestionable.

First comes the basic claim, that human value is real, *objective*, as opposed to made-up, *subjective*. The value of human life is a fact about the world: something we find, not something for us to decide. If the values people recognized were only subjective, then they could all have their own opinions about what should be counted as valuable. They could decide for themselves how much human beings mattered. Everyone could claim to be right; and nobody could presume to call somebody else wrong.

Objective values on the other hand are binding upon everyone and nobody can opt out. It is not true that there is nothing either good or bad but thinking makes it so.[25] If our values differ I shall have to call you wrong, and then I am not allowed to say that we can both be right. However tolerant I want to be, I must not say, 'I accept these moral demands as valid and binding for *me*; but it is quite all right

---

[25] *Hamlet*, II. ii. 252.

for you to decide that my top priorities are not important and perhaps not even good, for *you*.' Moral claims cannot be determined by people's willingness to be bound by them. Believers can surely hope that sceptics will agree with them so far, that the claims of persons are indeed objective.

To pronounce that the sanctity of a person's life is not only objectively real but *absolute* is not just another way of saying the same thing, but makes a further claim which may not necessarily follow. Affirming someone's real objective value and affirming someone's unqualified absolute value are both ways of taking the meaning of human life seriously, but they may not stand or fall together. Absolute value is not only compulsory for everyone as far as it goes, it is all or nothing. It cannot be weighed as more or less and there is no room for argument about how important it is, whether it always matters totally or maybe just to a certain extent.

The contrast now is with *relative* values, which however real and binding they are here and now may at some other time have to give way to different values. Circumstances alter cases and there is scope for flexibility. Relativists find that what is right and compulsory now does not stay put whatever happens. It does not follow that they can decide for themselves what they will count as good. Even though what is right or wrong may change, present value is still objectively real, not subjective.

It is not hard to give examples of how ethical demands can turn out to be real enough but variable. The moral assumption that 'Men must work and women must weep'[26] could once be accepted by men and women as common-sense realism, open to misuse on both sides but not unfair, because women were not strong enough to look after themselves and needed to depend on men to protect them. Unlimited motherhood was apt to be their inescapable vocation. Men therefore had the responsibility of being in charge and woman were bound to acquiesce, meekly or shrewdly.

---

[26]   Charles Kingsley, 'The three fishers'.

The conditions of everyday life have altered and the sub-ordination of women is neither fair nor realistic any more. Relativists who reject patriarchy now can understand that it had real value once. Early Christian leaders could see how inexpedient it would be for a woman to have authority over men, because the reputation of the church would be damaged.[27] But if Christians want to know what advice St Paul would give today, they can gratefully attend to his insight that 'In Christ there is neither male nor female.'[28]

If on the other hand values have to be absolute, what is wrong now was just as wrong in the past. Either our ancestors were at fault in the moral rules they established, or they were right and the people who want to change the rules now are wrong. Christians are often tempted to make a stand on ancient laws, particularly when they see the old ways as having biblical authority. Having rejected the idea that morality is for choosing, they also feel obliged to reject the idea that morality may change. They are afraid of the enticements of relativism, because they are afraid that moral clarity will disappear. They refuse to be satisfied with real but shifting values.

Children in Christian schools used to be taught to sing about how they might expect moral understanding to develop,

> New occasions teach new duties,
> Time makes ancient good uncouth.
> They must upward still and onward
> Who would keep abreast of truth.[29]

If that is relativism, is it so immoral?

Further reading

Emmet, Dorothy (1966) *Rules, roles and relations*. Macmillan.
Hare, R.M. (1952) *The language of morals*. Clarendon Press.
Hume, David (1740) *A treatise of human nature* Book III Part 1, end of Section i.

---

[27] *1 Timothy* 2.12.
[28] *Galatians* 3.23.
[29] From the hymn 'Once to every man and nation', itself part of a longer poem by James R. Lowell, 'The present crisis', which first appeared in print on December 11, 1845, in the *Boston Courier*.

Midgley, Mary (2006) 'On Dover Beach' *Philosophy*, April.

Moore, G.E. (1929) *Principia ethica*. Cambridge University Press.

Oppenheimer, Helen (1975) 'Ought and is' in *Duty and discernment*, ed. G.R. Dunstan. SCM Press (Reprinted from *Theology* June 1965) and see references there.

Oppenheimer, Helen (1983) *The hope of happiness: A sketch for a Christian humanism*. SCM Press.

Oppenheimer, Helen (1995/2003) 'Mattering, *Studies in Christian ethics*, 8:1 (reprinted in *Approaches to ethics nursing beyond boundaries* ed. Verena Tschudin. Butterworth Heinemann).

Oppenheimer, Helen (2006) *What a piece of work*. Imprint Academic.

Chapter 6

Valuing Lives

CLOWN:
What is the opinion of Pythagoras concerning wild fowl?

MALVOLIO:
That the soul of our grandam could haply inhabit a bird.

CLOWN:
What thinkest thou of this opinion?

MALVOLIO:
I think nobly of the soul, and in no way approve this opinion.

Twelfth Night, IV. ii.

Christians are particularly inclined to express their conviction that people are the primary bearers of value in terms of the *sanctity of life*, because they believe that human creatures are endowed with their value by their Creator. The reason why people are sacred is that they are made as images of God. For Christians, sacredness is a concept which applies first to God and derivatively to people. The sanctity of human life is the value and wonder of humanity made in God's image. A human being is an awe-inspiring creature, and 'creature' is being used now with its primary meaning, not referring dismissively to some alien animal, but indicating a life which depends on God the Creator.

When Christians find themselves in company with sceptical humanists who believe that human lives are truly valuable, who want to emphasize this in terms of the sanctity of life, the Christians should be pleased not ungracious. Believers and unbelievers can hardly expect to travel together indefinitely, but when agnostics or even atheists choose to call human existence sacred, believers ought to be glad of this convergence and not dogmatically repudiate it.

Anyone who is inclined to think in this way is likely to feel the force of the moral rule that human beings are not to be harmed or destroyed in any circumstances. If any moral claim is not only real but absolute, the claim of human life itself presents itself as the plainest example. Affirming the sanctity of life is a way of expressing the conviction that the life of a human being makes a total overriding demand upon anyone who cares about morality.

If the step is accordingly taken that human life is unconditionally sacred, it will appear that happiness and misery cannot count for much when it comes to decision-making, and inconvenience hardly at all. The only doubt is whether the life in question really is a human life. If there is *someone* here, that person exerts a moral claim which must be indisputable. People who adhere confidently to absolute value need a strong faith that these unqualified ethical duties which they recognize as binding will not confound them after all by turning out to be incompatible. Duties which appear irreconcilable should give them pause. Are they to obey the commandment 'Thou shalt not kill'[1] if it contradicts 'Do to others as you would have them do to you'[2]?

Ethical conclusions follow from religious beliefs about humanity, but Christians cannot simply read off their practical morality from their theology. To say 'This is a human being' makes a particularly strong moral claim on believers, but may not tell them definitely what duties they therefore owe. It is impressive to recognize every human being as a sacred soul, but when I have before me one of these human beings I am to consider as sacred, I may be none the wiser about what I ought to do or not to do. The idea of the sanctity of human life does not give much information about how to set about enhancing one another's living and dying.

People who do believe that each human life is sacred, but still hesitate to call this sacredness 'absolute', are in a better position to look at the circumstances and assess what their

[1]   *Exodus* 20.13.
[2]   *Luke* 6.31.

present duties are towards particular people. They are not obliged to make categorical pronouncements that every human life is inviolable. It may turn out that these real claims, which are never to be disregarded, may have different implications in different situations. The argument about what is right does not after all come to a sudden stop as soon as the question is posed.

On the contrary, practical problems begin here. People put an end to human lives, other people's and sometimes their own, for many reasons, malign and benign. It is being urged increasingly strongly that it is time to reconsider whether the sanctity of life may after all be an unhelpful slogan, which does not tell us much about what we ought to do. Does this argument-stopping notion of sacredness really add anything definite and conclusive to the practical moral imperatives we are bound to apply about doing people good and avoiding doing them harm? Maybe it only makes us stop thinking too soon.

In particular, the absolute ban, in the name of the sanctity of life, on helping someone in dire distress to choose to die sooner rather than later is coming to look like inhumanity rather than integrity. Excellent human skills in prolonging life have turned, for some people, into a threat. The commandment 'Thou shalt not kill' sometimes looks like a duty to 'strive Officiously to keep alive'.[3]

The case for changing the law to relieve the misery of people who seriously want to end their lives has lately been set out persuasively in a small book called *Easeful death*, by Mary Warnock and Elisabeth Macdonald.[4] Christians should at least be ready to ask whether life's sacredness always demands its relentless continuance. They may hold to that position, but they must answer the arguments. It is not enough simply to say 'Euthanasia! Hitler!' and refuse even to consider any options except leaving life and death in God's hands.

---

[3]   Arthur Hugh Clough (1819–1861), 'The latest Decalogue'.
[4]   Warnock & Macdonald (2008); see also Badham (2009). Both these books give the answer Yes.

Christians might have argued coherently in a different direction, in favour of helping a sacred soul in adversity on the way to a better life, if they had not been so accustomed to assume that the Everlasting has 'fixed His canon 'gainst self-slaughter'. The quotation is not from scripture but from Hamlet.[5] It is time to do some more careful thinking. Is the slope impossibly slippery all the way down from humane compassion towards hasty convenience, and eventually to Nazi death camps? The argument has become intractably polarized, stern high-principled believers versus merciful unbelievers. The rights and wrongs of the practical ethical problems about the end of life are more complex than that.

It should be pointed out that the last chapter of *Easeful death* leads into what a Christian may see as a mistaken turning, which may unnecessarily polarize the argument by putting Christians in a false position. The case this book makes for mercy-killing is brought to a close with just criticism of traditional dualism: so far, so good. Christians can be well content to relinquish the idea that people have separate souls distinct from their bodies.[6] But the argument moves smoothly on down a slippery slope of its own, towards doing away with the concept of the soul rather than reinterpreting it.

Easeful death seems to assume that anyone who wants to talk about souls must be committed to soul-and-body dualism. Christians are supposed to cling to a particular religious notion about what the sacredness of life means, which is holding them back from changing to 'a new perception of what it is to be human'.[7] They are saddled with an idea of the soul as a kind of entity which is sacred because it is 'especially God's responsibility.'[8] They are therefore hindered from attending to the urgent practical questions 'regarding our own responsibility for our own and other people's death'.[9] So the authentic hope this book offers that we may

---

[5]   *Hamlet*, I. ii. 131.
[6]   See above, Chapter 3; also Warnock & Macdonald (2008) , pp. 129f.
[7]   ibid. p.133.
[8]   ibid. p.134.
[9]   ibid.

all become more humane slithers into a requirement that in order to fulfil this hope we must simply set aside soul-language and God-language with it.

Provided that they notice that this slope is slippery, believers can find a firm place to stand where they do not have to forget about souls and let go of sacredness. First they can gladly abandon the idea of the soul as a ghost living in a machine.[10] Then they can keep hold of the idea of the soul as the complete human being, considered as a valuable whole. They need not divide a person into separate spiritual and physical sections in order to recognize someone who matters in God's sight.[11]

Yet understanding that every soul matters in God's sight still does not settle for believers the practical problem of how this child of God can be helped to approach death, without doing more damage to other children of God. The sacredness of every person sharpens the questions about people's responsibilities for one another rather than producing answers. Surprising as it may seem, the notion of life's sanctity is not after all the best place to make a stand. Mary Warnock and Elisabeth Macdonald need not be saying anything to shock Christians when they state, 'Life is not what is sacred, only lives.'[12]

There is still a large question-mark against assisted suicide which ought to count strongly with both Christians and sceptics: not the impiety of mercy-killing, but the recalcitrant practical difficulty, apt to be hastily under-estimated, of preventing its likely abuses. It is often not asked urgently enough whether 'this significant change to our law is safe.'[13] Practical doubts about mercy-killing have been lessened but not abolished. The residue which remains is not a superstitious fear of a tyrannical God, but a persist-

[10]   See above, p. 20.
[11]   See above, pp.20, 23f.
[12]   Warnock & Macdonald (2008) , p. 70.
[13]   Letter in *The Times*, November 5, 2008 from Lord Carlile of Berriew, QC.

ing worry about what may happen to vulnerable people if moral attitudes change.[14]

The peril is not so much a matter of a steep slope to Auschwitz, but rather of a slippery path towards a more insidious failure to uphold human worth. It would surely not be good for human beings to stop looking on suicide as dreadful. If a climate of opinion develops in which the accepted proper thing to do is to take one's leave in good time, seeds of submissive self-doubt may grow in the minds of people who do not want to die. 'It's selfish of me to go on living when I'm only in the way.' A 'gesture of impatience from those looking after them could be interpreted as a signal'.[15] Nor is it only people whose lives are anyway nearly over and people in desperate distress who might decide that they want to die, because they are fatally enticed by the tragic glamour of being more than half in love with easeful death.[16]

Nor should the danger be underestimated of expecting doctors to take on the role of ending their patients' lives. Doctors who repudiate the idea of mercy-killing are not 'playing God' but following an ancient and excellent medical tradition. They have been taught for two-and-a-half thousand years that their duty is to heal and not to kill. To require them to change their ways would be a revolution, with consequences not easily predictable. Already they are under unwonted pressure to bear in mind possible litigation when they make decisions. Could a doctor one day be sued, not for neglecting to cure his patient but for neglecting to kill her?

This question of assisted dying is a topical example of a recurrent practical difficulty of how to maintain the values we believe really matter, while allowing merciful exceptions to the rules we make for putting these values into effect: 'Never tell lies.' 'Never take other people's property.' 'Never put a marriage asunder.' 'Never destroy a human

---

[14] The argument is well set out by Nigel Biggar (2004), chapter 4, 'Slippery slopes'.

[15] Dunstan (1974), pp. 91–92.

[16] John Keats, 'Ode to a nightingale'.

life'. If 'sometimes', how can we decide *when*? Hard cases notoriously make bad law. When the cruelty of strict enforcement becomes evident, exceptions multiply and presently become no longer exceptional but normal.

It is time for something to be done about the distress of people who are being forced against their will to go on living: that is becoming increasingly clear. The answer is not obvious. The evidence from the experience of law-making in various countries is conflicting.[17] The careful arguments in *Easeful death* in favour of assisted dying should at least weaken pious prejudices, allowing believers to contribute constructively to the discussion.

If the arguments people of goodwill find themselves using about human happiness and misery turn out to be utilitarian arguments about consequences, they should not be alarmed. Religious moralists are too apt to scorn utilitarianism as a morality of mere expediency. They should remember that the contrary of 'expedient' is not 'virtuous' but 'inexpedient'. Surely it should alarm Christians a good deal more if considerations about God's will for human creature appeared to have nothing to do with considerations about their happiness. To keep looking hard at foreseeable consequences, far from being a betrayal of Christian principles, is a more effective policy than unthinking compliance for protecting the value of every human being.

Bishop Butler, as ever, was judicious about how to relate human wants to the law of God.[18] His emphasis was upon the ignorance of human beings, which forbids them to make people's immediate satisfaction their primary ethical concern. 'Always be kind' cannot be an adequate moral criterion for human beings, even if it may be for God who fully understands the problems and knows what real benevolence demands. For believers who share Butler's faith, conscience is a safer guide that knee-jerk kindness. 'Were the Author of nature to propose nothing to himself as an end

---

[17] See Warnock & Macdonald (2008), Introduction and e.g. pp. 84f. On the other side, see Biggar (2004), especially chapter 4 and the Conclusion.
[18] Butler (1729).

but the production of happiness, were his moral character merely that of benevolence: yet ours is not so.'

Unbelievers today are disposed to represent God the Lawgiver as not benevolent at all but rather as the great Tyrant. They are far from trusting the deliverances of the Christian conscience for moral guidance. If Christians insist on imagining God as the supreme Autocrat, whose ways are not our ways, whose instructions are definite but inscrutable, they will probably find themselves in perplexity and disorder. They would do better to take their stand on Butler's recognition that God may indeed be the great Utilitarian, who sees the whole picture, including the slippery slopes all around us.

The way God's will governs the morality of Christians is surely not by issuing plain edicts which leave people with nothing to work out for themselves. Whether Christians like it or not, their God does not dominate human decision-making but delegates dangerous responsibility to humanity.[19] What God seems often to say, to individuals and to legislators, is not simply 'Just say No' but 'Think'. To put one's mind to work on a hard problem in cooperation with other people is not disobedience. To make a decision to alleviate suffering in a risky untraditional way may be to act in the spirit of the Lord who healed on the Sabbath.

Mary Warnock and Elisabeth Macdonald are not so worried by slippery slopes and efficiently take to pieces many of the favourite arguments against assisted dying.[20] Mary Warnock has surely a better right than most people to set aside 'slippery slope' arguments, because the Committee of Inquiry into Human Fertilisation,[21] of which she was chairman, did set up a 'thus far and no farther' rule in another context, which has been respected rather than whittled away. The fourteen-day limit for experimenting upon embryos has so far held good.[22]

---

[19] Oppenheimer (1989).
[20] Warnock & Macdonald (2008), especially chapter 7.
[21] Warnock Report (1984); see Warnock & Macdonald (2008), p. 79.
[22] See below, pp. 62, 82.

They argue eloquently in conclusion that 'if we can come better to face our own mortality' we might see that 'easeful death may be the proper end for more people than we are at present inclined to believe'.[23] Christians may agree fully with this cautious suggestion. But still their politely cheerful dismissal of soul-language makes a counter-suggestible Christian fear that the perils of the slippery slope are likewise being dismissed too easily.[24] Butler's warning against short-term benevolence may still be needed.

Christians must join in weighing the arguments about whether the time has come for new legislation. The problems of setting the right limits can hardly be solved unless they are faced together with unprejudiced recognition of one another's concerns. What is at stake is not underlying dogmatic conviction about life's sacredness, but practical questions about how people can best honour and encourage one another, whether or not they express themselves in the terminology of sacredness. To put all the weight upon the sanctity of life is not the best way for Christians to commend the will of God nor indeed to discover it. It is even counterproductive, if it distracts attention from the real dangers.

Clear-headed attentiveness is a more constructive moral contribution than unshakable certainty. Addressing the dilemmas of medical ethics, G. R. Dunstan was wont to recommend the useful, and exacting, rule of *presumption for life*.[25] The moral law against taking human life is indeed compelling: but, in legal language, defeasible. A defeasible presumption holds: unless it is positively rebutted. Not killing people is the default position which it is a drastic decision to override.

Sometimes it may be understood that the problem does not arise because the principle 'Never take a human life' does not apply to this case. When a person is near death, the question may be whether there is still somebody here any more to whose wellbeing one can make any difference. It is not impious, and need not make a dangerous precedent, to

[23] Warnock & Macdonald (2008), p. 139.
[24] ibid. p. 133.
[25] e.g. Dunstan (1974), pp. 79–80.

decide to switch off the breathing machine. The criteria for action or inaction need not be different for Christians and sceptics.

Sometimes, when somebody is not dying yet, it is a still heavier responsibility whether or not to accept that this sufferer really wishes to die. Would it be right to help? It is looking more and more like a cruel injustice to forbid people to help. Must a woman's family face prosecution if they help her to die at the time she chooses? If we believe that she ought not to be compelled either to linger in distress, or to give up sooner than she wants while she is still in charge, it is important to make sure that her decision can responsibly be accepted as really hers.

People of goodwill arrive at acceptable decisions about particular cases in practice. It is harder to spell out and make generally available the criteria which make different cases different, excluding impulsive sentimentality or predatory self-seeking, on the one hand, and heartless rigidity on the other. The framing of laws capable of being applied to all manner of different situations is a more specialized task than doing one's best for one's own neighbour. Kindness to the one person in front of us may be cruel to unseen vulnerable people in the future. 'I didn't mean to' is an excuse but not a justification. Somebody must keep asking what effect a decision to cooperate with what this individual wants will have upon everybody else.

To do its job, a law must indeed be legalistic. It must 'show its workings' like a pupil doing a sum properly. Legal requirements need to be plain, lucid and firm, like the four-teen-day rule for experimenting upon embryos. 'You will probably get away with it' is neither just nor merciful. It is hard, but surely not beyond human ingenuity, to devise criteria for helping dying people which can establish for practical purposes the evident differences between one hard case and another.

The Director of Public Prosecutions has issued promising new guidelines[26] which do not make assisted suicide legal

[26] Reported in *The Times*, February 26, 2010.

but clarify the circumstances in which it should not incur punishment. The emphasis on 'the intentions of those providing assistance rather than the condition of those in distress' has been hailed as 'a victory for commonsense and compassion'. A leading article in *The Times*[27] has commended this judgement. At least the new guidelines deserve the chance to work better than the status quo. They offer an opportunity, neither to wield the blunt instrument of Parliamentary intervention, nor to insist upon a hard-hearted refusal to allow people to be helped

If people make the effort to listen to all sides, respecting one another's integrity and goodwill, refusing to think in slogans and constantly asking, 'What are we really doing, not just trying to do?' they might succeed in converging towards substantial agreement about how to value a person's life rightly. They may not be able to resolve their dispute about whether that person is a sacred soul, but they need not start there. Christians are not being disloyal if they start with the compassion which unbelievers comprehend, rather than making a stand upon the sanctity of life which hardens as a taboo. Affirming the holiness of human life is a way of drawing attention to the splendid significance of humanity, not a way of settling arguments about suicide and euthanasia.

Christians who want a biblical proof-text may remember that *inasmuch* as they try to serve their fellow human beings, it is God whom they are trying to serve.[28] They can engage wholeheartedly with their contemporaries in open-ended practical discussions about human happiness and unhappiness. They may find agreements with some sceptics and disagreements with some believers, without by any means betraying or undermining their conviction that human lives really are precious to God as well as to one another. What is required is neither a confident taking sides, nor an effort to perch precariously on a fence, but a commitment to follow where the argument leads. Making provisional decisions

---

[27]   ibid.
[28]   *Matthew* 25.40, 45.

about what seems best for now need not mean dithering or prevaricating.

Treading on a slippery slope may too easily be the first step towards collapsing at the foot. A better analogy for this kind of controversy might be a flight of slippery steps. People can move purposefully up or down with some control over their progress, still treading carefully not to lose their balance and fall. Believers and unbelievers can hope to make practical judgments together, exercising their common responsibility to relieve human suffering and find the least unhappy answers.

Further reading

Badham, Paul (2009) *Is there a Christian case for assisted dying?* SPCK.

Biggar, Nigel (2004) *Aiming to kill.* Darton, Longman & Todd.

Butler, Joseph (1729) Dissertation: 'Of the nature of virtue' Section 13.

Harries, Richard (2010), *Questions of life and death: Christian faith and medical intervention.* SPCK.

Oppenheimer, Helen (1989) 'Handling life' in *Doctors' decisions*, ed. G.R. Dunstan and E. A. Shinebourne. Oxford University Press.

Warnock, Mary & Elisabeth Macdonald (2008) *Easeful death: Is there a case for assisted dying?* Oxford University Press.

Chapter 7

Individual Persons

A little kindness — and putting her hair in papers — would do wonders with her.

Lewis Carroll, *Through the looking glass*, Chapter 9

Moral convergence between Christians and sceptics looks promising when Christians put aside their disapproval of utilitarianism and allow themselves to believe that God wants people to be happy. The argument soon becomes polarized again, because it is harder for Christians and sceptics to agree that God wants people to think for themselves. Secular humanists characteristically ascribe particular importance to the *autonomy* of the individual. Honourable non-believers may well find that their own self-reliant sovereignty has undeniable authority. They resolutely maintain their authentic independence and resist being pigeon-holed. Believers are apt to respond with a knee-jerk reaction against this human self-confidence which their contemporaries value so greatly.

The argument about assisted suicide brings this divergence to a head. People who want to change the law are taking up the cause of individuals who ought to have control over their own lives and deaths. How could one not be impressed by Terry Pratchett's brave claim: 'That is power. That is triumph. That is how a human being should die'?[1] But traditional Christians are unhappy with this and insist that 'human beings are not primarily autonomous but belong to God's care'.[2] They are fighting the wrong battle.

---

[1]   Terry Pratchett, reported in *The Times*, February 26, 2010.
[2]   Rolf (2010).

We need individualists, even though they can be awkward. They understand the worth of 'assertiveness' as a
positive virtue to be commended to diffident people; and
they repudiate the 'umbleness' of Uriah Heep. It is not con-
ceited for an eighteen-year-old to follow her own vocation
rather than modestly taking the course mapped out for her
by other people. Nor is it pig-headed for a member of a committee to vote according to his own conscience even if that
delays the proceedings. Christians cannot expect the meek
to inherit the earth if nobody is strong-minded enough to
stand up against injustice and maintain the right.

The right response to conscientious individualism is, 'So
far, so good'. Loyal Christians may rightly value independence of mind. What they cannot do is place the autonomy of
the individual at the centre of human value. The right place
to make their stand is upon people's mattering: to themselves indeed, and all along to one another. *We* is at least as
basic as *I*.[3] My value, like your value, is rooted in what I as a
particular individual mean to *us*.

'We were put into the world to do good to others' invites
the question, 'But what were the others put here for?' There
is no need to start a vicious regress. To respond, 'They, and
we, are put here for reciprocating goodness', can happily
establish, so to say, a virtuous circle. Negative self-denial
soon digs itself into a hole, but positive self-giving may
grow indefinitely. Self-giving and receiving might even be
expanded to infinity, so that a Christian could dare to find
an image here to illuminate the mystery of the Holy Trinity.

The prosaic terminology of 'mattering' is more promising
that the grander terminology of 'sacredness' for fixing people's attention upon their shared belief in the significance of
personal life. The value of persons is a main theme of ethics,
even the main theme. Whether or not people find it compelling to think of a person as a spiritual creature endowed
with absolute value, at least believers and non-believers
may agree with one another that here if anywhere there is
moral meaning. If anything matters, it matters whether

---

[3]   See above, p. 16.

there is someone here or not. The place to look for values is where they cluster around living conscious beings.[4]

When people who find meaning in life take their stand on the position called *humanism*, what they affirm is the value carried by any human being, considered as someone like themselves inhabiting the natural world.[5] The foundation of the moral stance called *personalism* is the value carried by each person, considered as someone who is living a life which matters.[6] What the point of view called *individualism* emphasizes is the special distinctiveness of every one of these particular and valuable persons.[7] Nobody is to be treated as simply replaceable by anybody else.

There is a happily enthusiastic frame of mind which gratefully adopts all these outlooks and includes them in a positive world-view. So much the better if these hopeful 'isms' can be welcomed under the umbrella of the Christian faith. Believers in God find a robust protection against the threat that everything which matters to us is going to perish in the end and our lives will all be of no avail, however significant we find them now. For Christians, the lasting individual value of all human persons is grounded in their creation in God's image. But before they can settle down in this faith and enjoy being Christian humanists, personalists and individualists, the ethical picture has to be pondered in a less optimistic light.

Though we can look for the meaning of our existence in the value which we believe is built into human creatures, it may not be so straightforward to find it. Pious people have to realise that they are as likely to find badness as goodness. Human beings are not always evidently worthwhile. The sacredness of life is an appealing idea, but its meaning cannot be hastily taken for granted. We can see a great deal wrong with most of these individual human persons. Their goodness looks too shaky to carry the whole weight of the value of God's creation. Should Christians after all persist in

[4]   See above, pp. 8, 35.
[5]   See above, p. 40; Oppenheimer (2006), pp. 26f.
[6]   See above, p. 43.
[7]   See above, pp. 44–45.

regarding mortal glory as a dangerous trap? Humanism seems presumptuous and personalism seems insecure; and individualism still appears the most equivocal of these three 'isms', splendid but also unsafe.

Individualism finds meaning in life by affirming and appreciating the distinctive worth of every human soul. Nobody, however ordinary or small, is to be treated as insignificant or lost in a crowd. Everyone matters. Christian individualists can be encouraged by the Gospel parables of the shepherd who goes after the one lost sheep and the housewife who hunts high and low for her missing coin and calls in her neighbours to celebrate with her when she finds it.[8] If individualism is gong to prove unreliable, it is its grandeur which can deceive us. Its worst is the corruption of its best.

The tyranny of a controlling group which sets individuals at nought is understood too well by school-children who encounter bullying, by minorities whose troubles are ignored, by people who live under totalitarian governments. The martyr is the prime example, but there is no need to be at risk of one's life to be made to understand what it feels like to be one person alone, up against a collective. To be too unimportant to count, to have one's opinions not even opposed but simply ignored, to be generally left out of what is going on, are ordinary experiences which ought to make good people wary of taking up moral positions which belittle the value of the individual.

But lessons can be too well learnt. It looks as if such brave confidence in the worth of human beings fatally underestimates the sinful condition of humanity. The secure independent person who stands up to be counted and refuses to be put down can go far astray. Autonomy is the kind of great good which slips easily into idolatry. Surely people who follow Christ are supposed to deny themselves, not to be assertive about their own importance?[9] Should Christians resist the allure of individualism and firmly rule it out of order after all, because 'the individual' is by nature

[8]   *Luke* 15. 4–10.
[9]   eg. *Mark* 8.34–5.

selfish and ought to be deprecated rather than affirmed? The conquest, not the appreciation, of the self can look like the main topic of Christian ethics, even the main concern of Christian theology.

From one major ethical point of view, each individual is sacred, including this one who is being neglected as insignificant or tiresome. That is the truth emphasized by people who take a strong stand against abortion. From another equally valid moral viewpoint, it is the selfishness of each individual which stands out, including the one I call 'I' who matters so much to me. Christians are to be found identifying themselves with both these convincing but seemingly contrary affirmations, 'hurrah' or 'boo' to valuable or selfish individuals, shouting them competitively like battle cries across the gap which separates believers from sceptics. From the secular side of the divide, both the positive and the negative slogans are to be heard shouted back.

As a humanist Christian who would like to bridge the gap between believers and unbelievers not widen it, I cannot simply adopt one of these slogans as evidently right and take it for granted that other people's approvals and disapprovals will match with mine. Because humanism is the starting-point I find congenial,[10] I am all the more bound to be realistic about the sinfulness of human beings and to take trouble not to make glib assumptions about the excellence of being 'I'. I can try to introduce a less belligerent discussion of the moral status of the individual by recommending a terminology which people with different presuppositions might adopt.

As a corrective both to humanist self-esteem on the one hand and to pious breast-beating on the other, I can resolve mostly to use 'this individual' colourlessly, for mentioning a specific person or thing, without praise or blame. 'This individual is quieter than the others.' 'It's too dark to distinguish individuals.' 'Each individual pupil has her own locker.' To speak of 'individualism' as an outlook on life still need not imply any immediate moral judgment whether

---

[10] See above, pp. 40, 67.

favourable or unfavourable, but can be useful for calling attention to the fact that some people mind more than others about being independent and self-sufficient. 'She hates to be humoured.' 'He works things out for himself.'

Sooner or later people have to start commending or blaming and then they need a less neutral vocabulary for contrasting better and worse approaches to human life. 'Personalism', as estimable, and 'atomism', as deplorable, are available as convenient terms for identifying different stances for approval or disapproval. Just because these labels are less confusingly ambivalent than either 'individualism' or 'humanism', they can be used less contentiously and controversially.

'Personalism' invites commendation, expressing the positive message, 'Up with persons'. A personalist is someone who maintains that persons, that is to say people, matter to themselves and to one another. Believers will base this confidence upon their belief that they matter especially to their Maker. 'Personalism' can then be suitably contrasted with 'atomism' which is more pessimistic and invites censure.

The *Concise Oxford English Dictionary* defines *atomism* as 'a theoretical approach that regards something as interpretable through analysis into distinct, separable, independent elementary components'. In the present discussion, the 'something' which is being interpreted is human experience and the keyword is 'independent'. Atomism is opposed here to 'holism'. Atomistic analysis treats people as separate units, and takes their lives apart in such a way that their relationships with one another are apt to get lost. 'Atomism' is a more accurate term than 'individualism' for directing critical attention to the besetting human habit of looking on ourselves as unattached self-contained items, without regard for anybody else.[11]

Human life is plagued by the tendency to disengage people from one another and let *us* go by default. Here is an enduring moral problem which is more practical and pressing than the theoretical problem of whether 'other minds'

---

[11] See below, p. 91.

exist. 'I all alone', after all, is the nightmare of a philosopher.[12] The strongest argument against solipsistic doubt may be that most people never feel it. What really is part of everybody's experience is 'I minding most about me'.

If this fault is named as atomism, there is less need to say 'boo' instead of 'hurrah' to the three 'isms', individualism, humanism and personalism. Their more encouraging meanings need not be set aside as dangerous. The trouble is not the conviction that individual human persons are valuable, far from it, but the separation of people from each other. What spoils the moral value of individuals is the dislocation of their relationships, when they succumb to the habit of making their separateness seem to be their most important characteristic. Their value to themselves obscures their value to others.

If people really were unconnected atoms, competition and even opposition would be people's ordinary stance. One person's gain would generally be someone else's loss. When 'I' is isolated like this from 'we', so that 'I' come first and everyone else afterwards, all my own particular wishes and enterprises, and even my highest aspirations, are bound to be based on egoism. Even my salvation may appear just as selfish as my passing whims. If I assume, however nobly, that my own immortal soul is my proper ultimate concern which takes priority over everything else, I am hindered from attending wholeheartedly to what will make you or anybody happy now or later

If 'the individual' keeps turning out to be a separate atom with a nucleus of essential selfishness, it is no wonder that Christians feel obliged to repudiate the prized notion of the valuable individual soul as a perilous snare. As usual, the answer must be to get the balance right. What matters is not to insist upon setting up a partisan 'either / or', but rather to keep affirming 'both / and',[13] not being surprised to find that people are regrettably corruptible and still positively worthwhile.

---

[12] See above, pp. 13ff.
[13] Oppenheimer (2006), p. 24.

Hoping to capture the right balance between the claims of oneself and the claims of others, Christian thinkers have tried to make accurate judgments by paying attention to the available vocabulary. A. M. Allchin emphasized the contrast Eastern Orthodox thinkers make between the individual and the person. The individual, he said, 'hugs his life to himself'; the person 'can only live through giving and receiving'.[14] David Jenkins in *The contradiction of Christianity* expressed himself still more strongly, asserting that 'the individual' is 'a dangerously dehumanizing myth. We are not individuals, we are persons.'[15] Likewise for J.A.T. Robinson in *The body*,[16] what mattered was not independent individuals but interdependent persons, finding themselves not separately but in communities.

Christians accordingly may be inclined to use 'person' to signify what we are to become as children of God and 'individual' to indicate what we falsely set ourselves up to be; but when they try to make this distinction work in practice they may not find it especially productive. To define one's terms is a help in arriving at truth, especially for clarifying what people have been trying to express all along; but confident definitions are apt to get out of hand. To brandish a definition is all very well if we can be sure that everyone is ready to identify the same distinctions and dutifully use them, but careful terminology cannot be expected to do all the work. For questions as difficult and contested as how to think about human nature, it is unpromising to build mighty arguments on words whose meanings are not yet fully agreed between the people joining in the discussion.

I can recommend useful ways of using words more accurately; but since I cannot count on everybody else co-operating in using the terminology I prefer, it is safer not to let my arguments depend upon my definitions. At least, for my own part, I can beware of ways of using language which push people into opposing camps. I need not work on the basis that unless 'individualism' is categorically

---

[14] Allchin (1978), p. 99.
[15] Jenkins (1976), p. 102.
[16] Robinson (1952).

admirable, the only alternative is to condemn and deplore it. I can attend to the different contexts which make diverse emphases important, where variegated judgments are needed to do justice to moral realities. I must try to be honest about human sinfulness, but I do not believe that Christian faith requires me to take the selfish self as the norm for fallen humanity. Christian humanism which appreciates God's creatures and is ready to find them 'very good' makes a more generous beginning than Christian gloom about human depravity. I can still keep hold of 'both / and'.

The particular peril of individualism is the easy slide into atomism. A good awareness of the particular individuality of oneself and other people can go wrong. Too straightfor-wardly it can begin to look as if being someone implies, not just being distinct, but being apart from other people. Because thinkers who embark on a philosophical argument about the nature of persons are so tempted to make a start with the solitary individual, neither caring nor cared for, it often needs to be reiterated that such an egotist would not be a characteristic human being but would indeed be an aberration. Nobody really begins here.

This argument about what it means to be someone cannot remain an intellectual enquiry into the nature of a person, belonging to the subject called 'theory of knowledge'. The question soon shifts into ethics, a moral enquiry into the values which cluster around personal life.[17] 'Ought' cannot be left out of 'is' for long. It matters morally as well as intellectually to reject atomism as a way of thinking about persons.

People's lives are not naturally separated. The ways they are connected comprise all kinds of association, from plain business dealings to profound belonging. The ordinary ethical glue which keeps all these from falling apart is trust. In a way, trust is a more basic moral concept even than love. The possibility of some basic reliance upon other people is a sine qua non of living a human life. However generously good people may want to behave to one another, ordinary

---

[17] See above, pp. 66–67 and note 4 there.

trust is where they have to start. The idea of a society of wholly undependable individuals is not only hellish: it is nonsensical.

For any creatures who live in societies and communicate intentionally with one another, predictability and truth-telling must logically be standard. Falsity and lying must be deviations. Although sin damages and even destroys the good patterns of human relationship, 'All men are liars' still cannot be more than a half-truth. This requirement is an example of the useful philosophical idea of a conceptual necessity.[18] If anything like the human life we know is to work, there must be a presumption of trust, though that presumption may be rebuttable. Trustful communication may have to carry many exceptions, but they must be acknowledged as exceptions. Prevalent as deceit may turn out to be, it is essentially parasitic upon honesty.

Professor H.L.A. Hart in *The concept of law*[19] put the necessity for trust in its proper ethical setting. The rules people count as moral laws cannot take just any shape, imposing random obligations and prohibitions. He 'insisted that in all moral codes there will be found ... requirements of truthfulness, fair dealing, and respect for promises'. He enumerated 'certain very obvious truisms about human nature' which could be the foundation of 'a core of indisputable truth in the doctrines of Natural Law'.

To give truthfulness such a central ethical place is the start of moral problems not the answer to them. To say 'NEVER tell lies' looks too simple. People usually believe that the presumption in favour of truth-telling is, in legal terminology, 'defeasible'.[20] If so, they will have a great deal of work to do to sort out what duties and permissions follow. What exceptions to truthfulness are allowable? Are some exceptions positively required? Is trust always admirable, or is it sometimes culpably naive? What means can people devise for making the most of trust and shoring it up when it wobbles?

---

[18] See Oppenheimer (1975), and Note 18 there, pp.131–132.
[19] See Hart (1962), p. 176.
[20] See above, p. 61.

Human beings have devised workable stratagems for making it clear when they are definitely committing themselves, especially the 'performative' use of language when speaking becomes doing. To utter specific words can be, not simply making a statement about the world, but enacting something in the world.[21] By saying, 'I promise', or 'I will',[22] or by putting their signatures to documents, people are not just saying something about what the facts are now. They are binding themselves for the future in recognizable ways which generally work.

Human beings have not succeeded so well in devising satisfactory honest procedures to safeguard the important right to keep silent and refrain from making any statement at all.[23] What is someone to do when confronted by an aggressive or careless question? Telling a lie in self-defence should be permissible, if using violence in self-defence is taken to be permissible. Telling a lie so as not to betray somebody else's secret is still more justifiable, even obligatory. An out-and-out lie in an emergency may do less damage to the fabric of human reliability than an easy habit of telling 'white' lies in everyday life, which people suppose is quite acceptable but which makes it impossible to trust one another. There is more to be said than many upright moralists suppose for equivocation, which is a challenge to listen carefully to what has and what has not been stated. People who on principle will not say anything which is actually false cannot rightly claim that this is truthfulness, but at least they are making an effort not to fill the world with dangerous fog.[24]

The ethics of sincere communication, far from being peripheral, should be taken into consideration among people's central concerns. On the one hand human beings are distinct individuals, who may not always wish to reveal their private lives to one another. On the other hand they are not independent individuals, who may as well go their sep-

---

[21] See Austin (1962).
[22] See Oppenheimer & Montefiore (1971).
[23] See Baker (1970), pp. 89–90; Oppenheimer (2006), chapter 13 'Telling'.
[24] See Oppenheimer (2000).

arate ways. To appreciate the human ability to share their experiences honestly, to be linked to one another by promises and vows, to give pledges which they can be expected to keep, is a fundamental aspect of understanding what it means to be someone, to be a person among other persons.

Further reading

Austin, John (1962) *How to do things with words*. Oxford University Press.

Hart, H.L.A. (1962) *The concept of law*. Oxford University Press: p.176 and Chapter 9.

Oppenheimer, Helen with Hugh Montefiore (1971) 'Vows', appendix to *Marriage, divorce and the church,* The report of the Commission on the Christian doctrine of marriage. SPCK.

Oppenheimer, Helen (1978) 'Fidelity' The Mary Sumner Lecture 1978.

Oppenheimer, Helen (2000) 'The truth-telling animal' in *Dumbing down*, ed. Ivo Mosley. Imprint Academic.

Oppenheimer, Helen (2006) *What a piece of work*. Imprint Academic: Chapters 3 and 13.

Chapter 8

Sacred Souls

I will give thanks unto thee, for I am fearfully and wonder-fully made: marvellous are thy works, and that my soul knoweth right well.

My bones are not hid from thee: though I be made secretly, and fashioned beneath in the earth.

Thine eyes did see my substance, yet being unperfect: and in thy book were all my members written;

Which day by day were fashioned: when as yet there was none of them.

Psalm 139.13–16

Since *we* is more basic than *I* alone, and people's lives depend upon relationships with one another, the question arises both for believers and sceptics, who is to be included, as someone who belongs among *us*? How far does the human community extend?

Christians must engage with their contemporaries in asking questions about when a human life begins. The development of the medical possibility of safe abortion has made it an urgent moral problem whether putting an end to a pregnancy can sometimes be right. Granted that it is dire to kill a fetus and that it is dire to ruin a grown woman's life: which is worse? Whether this developing creature is a sacred soul in God's eyes will surely make a difference to the answer. Christians must consider the sanctity of a human life as at least a relevant consideration.

The problem of abortion is not therefore easily solved, if only we have faith. Even if we think we understand what 'sacredness' means,[1] and even if we grant for the sake of

---

[1]   See above, Chapter 6.

argument that every human being is sacred, it still turns not to be obvious when the sacredness of a particular human life is supposed to begin. What can our responsibilities be to a potential person who is not living in the world yet, who has never lived in the world and who may never become an actual person at all? Both Christians and sceptics need to pursue the enquiry about the dawn of personhood because of its relevance to practical problems about human duties. The enquiry is also important for the light it could shed on human puzzlement about what it means to be 'someone'.

The controversy about whether terminating a pregnancy is morally equivalent to killing a child is not well pursued by taking sides forthwith, setting the human rights of a woman against the divine right of this new life which has come into existence, as if *either* one *or* the other is to be counted as valid. It is high time for both 'pro-life' and 'pro-choice' to give more credit to each other's integrity. Each side could try harder to bring imagination as well as logic to bear on what the other is saying, looking for understanding rather than victories.

The presenting problem is what individuals ought to do or refuse to do in particular circumstances. The people who are called upon to make decisions are not only the women themselves who are to bear the children or not bear them, but also their families, husbands and partners who can back them up or hinder them; the doctors and nurses whose skills they need; and beyond them the legislators who must decide what may or may not be allowed for the sake of the common good. All these people have to take some responsibility for the life or death of potential human beings.

Alongside all these are moralists who are not themselves at the moment directly confronted by pressing ethical choices. Their task should not be to preach, but to clarify the minds of the people who have to act.[2] Anyone who has influence upon other people's opinions ought to be alert to the immediate benefits and harms for particular individuals,

---

[2]   This chapter is particularly indebted to the work of G.R. Dunstan, whose thinking about medical ethics was founded upon a profound respect for the 'practitioners'.

and must be asked to look further, to consider what effects permissions and prohibitions will have upon public understanding of what makes lives worthwhile.

Granted that human life is to be protected, where are the limits are to be set? The law has been framed to allow an abortion when a fetus is likely to be seriously disabled. What effect will this have on our notions about disability? Is 'normality' to be treated as a value which can trump every other value? May normality become a tyranny, as if a disabled child were the new kind of illegitimate child who ought never to have been born, who having arrived in this world is only too likely to suffer disapproval and discrimination? Are we really entering upon a 'culture of death', doing away with people just because their existence is inconvenient?

But on the other hand, 'pro life' must be asked just as urgently to try to imagine what sort of life is being so confidently accepted on behalf of people who are born disabled and for their families. If someone is too impaired to share in ordinary human hopes and join in ordinary human living, it may well appear that it would have been better for everyone if that baby had never been born. Would it have been wrong to intervene in time to prevent that potential existence from ever taking shape, before that human being had become what Tom Regan called 'the subject of a life',[3] before there was someone there at all who could mind about living or dying?

Christian moralists need not claim the moral high ground as their special domain. They need not imagine themselves as confronting hordes of hostile relativists who want to get rid of well-tried traditional moral convictions and install dangerous permissiveness. Instead Christians can hope to join with other people of goodwill in well-informed and constructive debate concerning what to believe about persons, where to find them and what to do for them. The discussion must be both theoretical and practical.

---

[3]   See above, p. 44.

Recognizing unreservedly that here is a living being which is human may not mean affirming forthwith that here is *someone*. Suppose that the presence of 'someone' is not a matter of *all* or *nothing*. It may turn out that the full value of a human life is not given all at once, at a moment when the sperm and the ovum unite, but develops gradually. It is a responsible conviction, maintained by distinguished Christian moralists,[4] that whether a living being is a person, or is not a person, really is a difference of degree rather than a difference of kind.

The suggestion that a potential person is not actually a person yet should not be treated as if it were a weak and dangerous concession to unprincipled people who want to justify what they wrongly want to do. The belief that the soul develops gradually is as responsible a position as the all-or-nothing stance that abortion kills a child. The pro-life slogan, 'human life is sacred from the moment of conception' is not a plain and basic axiom for Christians to uphold and defend along with the Creeds, doubted only by wobbly liberals who probably doubt the Creeds too.

The history is more complex than many loyal Christians feel obliged to assume.[5] Ancient authority does not speak with one voice. *Scripture* is almost silent. *Tradition* is not, after all, unanimous. There is also a strong tradition, a Catholic tradition, which goes back to St Thomas Aquinas who learnt it from Aristotle, that the soul does not arrive suddenly at conception but develops gradually through the months. Christians therefore may and must bring the authority of *reason* to bear; and reason suggests that the medical ethic which makes most sense, both for common-sense morality and for theological loyalty, is that the fetus, growing into a person, ought to have increasing protection. The statement that the soul develops gradually is not a negative denial of its sacredness but a positive recognition of its

---

[4]   Besides G.R. Dunstan, notable examples are John Habgood and
       Richard Harries (e.g. Habgood 1993, chapter 7; 1998; Harries 2010,
       and his biography by Peart-Binns, 2007, chapter 21).
[5]   See Dunstan (1990), e.g. p.5.

significance: a stance which needs and deserves careful defence.

If *someone* develops in stages, the story starts with an earlier state of affairs before there is anyone there at all. Before conception, there are living cells made of human DNA, but neither the sperm nor the ovum is a human being who might or might not be aborted. To use contraception to prevent sperm and ovum from uniting is a different moral decision with its own arguments. Contraception, whether moralists forbid it, allow it, or recommend it, is not a kind of abortion, because until sperm and ovum are joined nobody could suppose that there is a particular victim who is being killed rather than cherished.

Conception is indeed the *first stage* of a new human life. To make a stand here and draw a line at the 'moment of conception' is undoubtedly attractive; but becomes less so when it is made clear that conception is not really a specific identifiable moment. Fertilization is itself a process and the arrival of sacredness already turns out to be gradual.

Then *secondly*, once fertilization is complete there is indeed a growing human being. This early stage of development has lately been called the 'pre-embryo'.[6] It is not specious to argue that a human pre-embryo is still not *someone*. Before legalistic confidence takes over that the strictest view must be right, commonsense deserves a hearing. It seems that over 40% of fertilized ova never implant and never develop into embryos, let alone babies.[7] Once implantation has happened, it will still be about fourteen days before the embryo begin to develop the physical structures on which conscious experience will be based. If these very early human lives are already sacred, does that mean that they are *people*? If they perish, will they arrive in heaven, taking priority over all the sociable apes and beloved dogs? This is not an ungenerous argument that 'heaven would be over-stuffed with such souls' as a review in *Crucible*[8] suggested. It is an inability to believe seriously in a heaven most of whose

---

[6] Warnock Report (1984).
[7] See Cook (1995), p. 131.
[8] 2007, July issue, p. 55.

inhabitants, when they were alive on earth, were no more aware than plants of anything whatsoever, still less capable of loving anybody.

To accept that early embryos are not yet persons does not mean classifying them forthwith as mere objects. A dictum of Bishop Butler deserves to be heeded: 'Everything is what it is and not another thing'.[9] Scientists, and people who might benefit from their work, have to attend to the ethical question whether this kind of wonderful being which is a 'pre-embryo' may be killed for medical research. This is related to, but distinct from, the argument about aborting a formed fetus. Many responsible people believe that reverence for the humanity of pre-embryos, which have not yet developed any capacity for awareness, allows them to be respectfully used to relieve human suffering, in something like the way in which reverence for the humanity of a corpse, who has no capacity for awareness any more, is taken to be compatible with respectfully dissecting it.[10]

This exercise of moral responsibility is not 'playing God', but can be a proper use of the rationality given to human beings by their God, whom we may well describe as a God who delegates.[11] Scientific study of the beginning of the process by which every human baby has developed from a cluster of cells may encourage a reverent wonder at the marvel of creation, which indeed is not uncharacteristic of people who work in this speciality.

The *third stage*, at about fourteen days, is when the 'primitive streak', the foundation of the nervous system, appears and there is definitely *a human being* here. The case for 'pro life' gains ground now. Fourteen days has been agreed as the moment after which using embryos for research must be forbidden by law.[12] Can this chosen but not arbitrary point be morally recognized as the birth of the human soul? However chary one is of magic moments, at least it can be said that from now on destroying a fetus is definitely killing a

---

[9]   Butler (1726).
[10]   Oppenheimer (1989), p. 212.
[11]   ibid., pp.205–207, 210; see above, p. 60.
[12]   See above, p. 62.

human being. The onus of proof is on anybody who wants to treat this particular human life as expendable or to deny that it is sacred in whatever way human beings are sacred.

If it does indeed appear that the moral status of the embryo develops like this from one stage to another and that the unborn baby is a potential person but still not yet an actual person, that is no justification for brushing aside the value which belongs to it already and disregarding the tragedy of abortion. The destruction of an embryo is not well compared with the removal of an inflamed appendix. It is more like killing young enemy soldiers who are invading one's country.

Though avoidance of all violence is a noble ideal, self-defence is generally taken to be a valid reason for a warlike response. Most people recognize that war is a tragedy. Some people, but evidently not all, have the vocation to be pacifists. People may make sacrifices on their own behalf but it is a heavy responsibility to refuse on principle to defend other people from harm, or to blame them for defending themselves.

To honour the marvellous creature a fetus is does not mean treating it as so sacred that nothing else counts. Its moral importance may be authentic without being absolute.[13] People who are not pacifists and are willing to let human beings be killed on their behalf have no right to condemn abortion out of hand. It may be the least of evils, when to let this potential life develop into consciousness would be life-wrecking for people who are already aware of being alive. The principle of *presumption for life* is strong but sometimes rebuttable.[14] The plainest examples of rebuttal are when a woman has been raped, or when the child is going to be too disabled to find life worthwhile.

One can tell various stories and slant them in various ways. The present point is not the detail, but the assertion that if non-pacifists can be right about justifiable homicide, then 'justifiable feticide' should count as an example of it. This assertion must immediately be balanced by the clear

[13] See above, p. 54–55.
[14] See above, p. 61 and n. 25 there.

recognition that it is always wrong to treat human life as simply expendable. At least it cannot be right to destroy a fetus merely for convenience. Even when it appears that abortion is best for everyone, we must still feel the pity of it.

Fourthly, the stage when the baby 'quickens' in the womb has been traditionally recognized as a significant phase in the development of a fetus into a person. Aristotle's biological teaching, as adopted into Christian thought by St Thomas Aquinas, declared that the embryo developed first as a kind of plant and then as an animal, and that eventually it was animated with the God-given rational soul. 'Quickening' was the point when the human person was ensouled and came to life. It followed, not only that early abortions might be tolerated, but also that the final authority on whether this crucial stage had arrived did not belong to controlling experts, whether doctors or priests, but to the mother herself who could feel her baby move.[15] Abortion was not made a crime in England until 1803. It was not until 1868 that Pope Pius IX ruled that abortion is wrong from the moment of conception. When upholders of a woman's choice refuse to allow men, often celibate men, to decide moral questions for women, they are not after all repudiating a unanimous tradition.

People no longer take 'quickening' to be fundamentally important, but there is an equivalent stage in the development of the fetus which is medically significant. At a time which nowadays may be long before 'full term', the fetus is *viable*. If it is born, it may live. It makes sense to think of it now as an 'unborn child'. To terminate the pregnancy, besides being increasingly drastic for the mother, looks more and more like killing a baby. The medical staff who a moment ago were trying to terminate a pregnancy may find themselves urgently taking care of a breathing infant. Once the fetus is viable, 'pro-life' can confidently maintain that abortion is wrong, although they may well except therapeutic abortion to save the mother so that both lives need not be lost. If, in what one hopes are rare circumstances, there is no

---

[15]   Angus McLaren 'Policing pregnancies' in Dunstan (1990), p. 203.

chance of positively choosing life, the moral question becomes not 'May we kill?' but 'Who must die?'

Strangely enough, 'pro life' and 'pro choice' can now begin to converge and this fourth stage turns out not to be more controversial, but less. Religious people who believe in sacred souls and secular moralists who believe in human rights can find themselves able to agree that there is another person here, someone else in addition to the mother, whose interests may conflict with hers. A doctor has two patients to consider, not only one. The law of the land is now properly concerned. To destroy this human being is evidently a kind of homicide, justifiable or not. To protect its life with penalties is not interfering in people's private affairs.

The *fifth* and ultimate stage is birth. A new person has arrived in the world. There is certainly a separate human being here, whose own distinct status the law recognizes and protects. People who argue for abortion do not generally go on to argue for infanticide. At least from birth onwards, the presumption for life looks steady.

It may be pointed out that this line which is drawn to mark the arrival of a new person in the human community is still a fuzzy line even here. If independent existence is a criterion for having human rights, a newborn baby is hardly more independent than a nine-month fetus. An embryo is already entirely viable in its own way, living and developing in its natural habitat, as long as it is not attacked. An older child, or even a fully-grown man or woman, is hardly viable if removed from nourishment, shelter and care.[16]

There is a potentially slippery slope from abortion, to infanticide, to plain homicide, to euthanasia. Are all or none of these kinds of killing always culpable? It is tendentious to call abortion child-murder. Many morally responsible people judge that terminating a pregnancy may not be equivalent to killing a child and may sometimes be considered a necessary evil. Fuzzy lines are inconvenient, but when reality is fuzzy definite practical decisions still have to be made somehow.

---

[16] Oppenheimer (1989), p. 207.

Looking back over the whole argument, it may appear that the presumption for life has been fatally weakened. It looks as if, in the earlier stages of pregnancy at least, 'pro choice' has prevailed. Rather than staying stuck in the assumption that the only way to proceed from here is to keep on arguing about rights, the rights of a woman versus the rights of the fetus, Christians had better move on from asking about allowing and forbidding. If they consider instead whether what they believe about God's grace may shed light on the meaning of parenthood, they may hope to pose the questions women face over choosing or refusing to be mothers in a less argumentative and antagonistic manner. They might enlarge their understanding of what it means to be a human person.

The bringing of children into the world has ethical significance which goes beyond the physiological facts which biologists can describe or the rules which lawyers can formulate. Becoming somebody's parent means more than a medical or legal history. This conviction is part of what believers are trying to express when they affirm the sacredness of life from its very beginning. They may be feeling after the idea that the way children matter to their parents in something like the way that people matter to God.

The argument about abortion could readily be pursued from here in a 'pro life' direction. On the authority of the Gospel, God's Fatherhood is the best image of God's grace. When the unconditional love of God is described by likening it to the sustenance, physical and emotional, which human parents are trusted to give to their children, it is hardly surprising if the question of ending a pregnancy is taken to be answered for Christians before it has even been asked. How could any Christian woman who believes that God will never abandon His children even consider aborting her baby?

Another morally valid way of comparing human parenthood with God's may lead in a different direction. Believers recognize their entire dependence upon the grace of God. They cannot claim any rights of their own. They can compare this with the way an undeveloped human being grows in entire dependence upon the grace of its mother. The life of this new person comes through her or not at all. The embryo becomes *someone* by its mother's gift.

It is part of the meaning of grace that it is freely given and uncompelled. People can long for grace, hope for it and even expect it, but they cannot demand it as a right. Traditionally children have been taught to be grateful to their parents for bringing them into the world. It does not make sense to honour people who are grace-givers unless we think of them as having some choice in the matter. A baby depends upon the blessing of its mother to grow to be a person; and it is something like a logical mistake to try to make blessing compulsory.[17] To recognize that a woman may refuse to continue this pregnancy is to dare to recognize that divine responsibility is delegated to this woman. It must be counted as a real option for her to say not Yes but No.

For many reasons, good and bad, a woman may be unwilling and perhaps unable to bless this baby into humanity. Because she is human, she is capable both of selfishness and of generosity and the choices she makes are part of the ethical mixture of human life. Rather than insisting upon women's rights, Christians who affirm women's choice would do better to argue that parenthood is a *calling* which people have no right to force upon other people.

A woman can decline to become the mother of the fetus she is carrying. The law of the land now will generally back her up. It is for her to face the hard question whether in God's eyes she may be refusing a vocation. She is very likely not saying, 'I don't want this baby and it is my right to decide that I won't have it.' She may be saying, 'I simply can't cope.' If she believes in God she may be beseeching God somehow to take over and have mercy. But indeed she may truly be affirming with open eyes, 'I believe that it is better to stop this possible new person from coming into existence.' Christians need not refuse to consider this judgment as a valid moral stance. At least they need not take for granted that what God wants is that as many people as

[17] cf Oppenheimer (1991a).

possible shall be born, however much damage they are likely to do.

Both 'pro life' and 'pro choice' need to shift from emphasizing rights to emphasizing supported responsibility. In combating the legalism of 'pro-life', 'pro-choice' has been inclined to absolve women from accountability and to suggest that pregnancy is an unlucky crisis which might happen suddenly to anybody, like catching measles or falling downstairs. Conception happens because of choices: to say Yes to this man, to take no precautions, to go along with natural inclinations. Because men have been too much inclined to blame women and punish them, the moral pendulum has swung the other way. Not wanting to be 'judgmental' or to suggest that a baby is a penalty for transgression, people of goodwill make light of human responsibility, as if getting rid of blame implied getting rid of ethical meaning altogether. However justifiable and even urgent the decision to end this growing life may be, it is still seemly to take abortion seriously, to feel the pity of it and to mourn it as a tragedy.

In a notable article,[18] Judith Jarvis Thomson developed a comparison between a pregnant woman and a kidnap victim who finds herself joined to a famous violinist whose kidneys are failing. The woman with exceptional generosity may allow the situation to continue, but the intruder has no right to demand that her body shall be used to save his life. Professor Thomson almost made the move from the rights of the fetus to the 'special kind of responsibility'[19] which belongs to the woman who is its mother; but the impression remains that what she means by responsibility is still legalistic. She went straight on to imagine a situation where 'people-seeds drift about in the air like pollen' and a householder who does not take reasonable precautions to exclude them turns out to be responsible for letting them in. As a defence of abortion, this analogy is counter-productive. Indeed it brings out the inadequacy of reducing motherhood to a mishap. However decisive the reasons can be for

[18]　Thomson (1971).
[19]　ibid. p. 64.

not letting this fetus live to be someone, a fetus is no passing stranger, a 'person-seed' which 'drifts in and takes root.'[20] The 'special kind of responsibility' of being the one who could bring a new person to birth really is special, even though it may have to be repudiated.

Whatever a woman decides to do about her dilemma, it is far from Christian charity to leave her to bear her responsibility unaided. If the argument could cease to be so polarized, she could receive the practical support of the people who respect her choice, without having to lose touch with the people who emphasize the pity of it. She needs comfort, not only in the newer sense of 'consolation' but in the old sense of 'strengthening'. It is not enough to offer counselling, as if that were a magic spell against unhappiness. Moral sensitivity towards someone who has to make a big decision needs to be expressed as available continuing help, if she is not to be pushed into making her choice one way or the other, not because it is the best but because she cannot see any alternative.

Moralists who were wasting less energy on blaming each other might be more able to attend to both sides of the case. The question is not settled but it should be less unmanageable. On the one hand, there is the reality of people's inability to cope, and particularly the fearful harm which looking after a gravely disabled child can do to a whole family. On the other hand, there are the voices of people who might have been aborted who find themselves glad to be alive. There are the consciences of doctors whose own valid vocation is still to preserve life not destroy it. There are spreading circles of concern, reaching people unknown to the ones faced with the immediate problem, a generation who will live their lives in whatever climate of opinion is created in the long term by the short-term decisions being made now.

What more could be done to provide conditions in which this problem would not arise so often and so acutely, in other words, to pre-empt it before it began? At least ethical education ought to be a priority, starting in time to

[20]   ibid. p. 59.

strengthen the next generation both with well-informed prudence and also with well-thought-out morality. Children should be encouraged to ask themselves and other people what sort of life is most worth living and what they can do about it. They need to be shown by precepts and examples how the adults they are going to become can best handle the responsibilities they may have to carry and learn to look after one another.

The point of looking at the problem of abortion in such detail has not been to work out in practice just how the notion of sacredness ought to be applied to varying situations, nor to settle in theory a definition of what the 'sacredness' of a soul means. The immediate point has been to establish that mattering does not have to be an all-or-nothing notion. To take seriously how special people are does not mean thinking of their significance as an indisputable claim arriving instantly, all complete, at a particular moment. To refrain from insisting that every human embryo must already be a new person could open people's minds to ask more promising questions about what it does means to be someone and how it matters.

Further reading

Cook, E.D. (1995) 'Abortion' in Atkinson, J.D. and D.H. Field, ed. (1995) *New dictionary of Christian ethics and pastoral theology*.

Dunstan, G.R., ed. (1990) *The human embryo: Aristotle and the Arabic and European traditions*, the report of the Constantinus Colloquy, a multi-disciplinary conference held at Exeter University in 1988. University of Exeter Press.

Ford, N.M. (1988) *When did I begin?* Cambridge University Press.

Oppenheimer, Helen (1989) 'Handling life' in *Doctors' decisions*, ed. G.R. Dunstan and E. A. Shinebourne. Oxford University Press.

Oppenheimer, Helen (1991a) 'Blessing' in *The weight of glory: Essays for Peter Baelz*, ed. D.W. Hardy and P.H. Sedgwick. T. & T. Clark.

Oppenheimer, Helen (1992) 'Abortion: A sketch for a Christian view', *Journal of Christian ethics* 5:2.

Thomson, J.J. (1971) 'A defense of abortion', *Philosophy and public affairs*, 1:1.

Warnock Report (1984) *Report of the Committee of enquiry into human fertilisation and embryology*. Her Majesty's Stationery Office.

Chapter 9

One and Many

The devil 'always sends errors into the world in pairs—
pairs of opposites'.
                    C.S. Lewis *Mere Christianity*, p. 147.

Being *someone* generally implies being in touch with other
people. Once the philosophical 'problem of other minds'
has rolled away like a dark cloud,[1] we, not just I on my own,
have profitable lines of argument to follow together about
human flourishing. There are live ethical problems about
communication and the ways it can fail, understanding and
misunderstanding, independence and interdependence,
individualism and its ambivalence, the values and the
weaknesses of people and groups. In these explorations,
Christians and sceptics can co-operate.

The practical menace of *atomism* remains more persistent
than the theoretical menace of solipsism.[2] It is easy enough
to believe that the world is indeed full of people. It is harder
to move from facts to values and grasp how people are
morally linked together. Because the 'self' is inclined to selfishness, human beings often behave as if they were all
separate items. whose independence mattered more than
the ties between them.

Christians have been taught to see this danger especially
clearly. Unfortunately, having repudiated self-centred
detachment, they proceed to claim the ethical high ground
as their own. It feels morally safe to cast down the mighty
individual and exalt instead the community of God's

---

[1]   See above, e.g. pp.14ff.
[2]   See above, pp. 70ff.

people. Should Christians accordingly repudiate the sinful *one* and concentrate entirely on the *many*?

Some of the most insidious errors which afflict human thinking come from proving too much, from over-correcting a false emphasis. Egocentric individualism is evidently a false emphasis which does need to be repudiated. *We* really is as basic as *I*; it is not good for humankind to be alone; we do find ourselves by belonging.[3] So far, so good; but if these insights are over-emphasized in their turn, the threat of individualism gives way to the contrary threat of group tyranny which has been there all along.[4]

People may correct idolatrous self-assurance only to fall under the domination of the collective. Overweening communities are as dangerous as overweening individuals. This is a lesson which twentieth century people learnt a hard way, by seeing for themselves what brutal regimes emerged inexorably out of the early optimism of both Fascist and Communist societies.

Too clearly, even the Christian Church has not been free from the corruptibility of groups. Churches in control have been as guilty as political movements of distorting idealism into tyranny, from the conscientious cruelty of the Inquisition to the self-righteous governance of puritans. 'See how these Christians love one another', first remarked in good faith, has notoriously turned into devastating irony.

Communities which have left behind the horror of burning heretics alive for the good of their souls may still not have their emphasis right. Instead of developing considerate goodwill, they remain prone to complacent domination. 'This is what you need and if you don't see it that way you must repent.' Moralists who count themselves as loyal members of benign groups ought to beware of making well-meaning confident jumps to insidiously oppressive positions. If they fail to put themselves in other people's places in order to see what they see, the other people will hardly be able to recognize the groups as benign.

---

[3]   *Genesis* 2.18; see above, pp. 16, 73.
[4]   See above, p. 68.

People upholding 'community' make 'individual' into a 'boo-word,'[5] but the people who still want to use it as a 'hurrah-word' stubbornly go on believing that individuals are important after all. Surely each person does matter too much to be routinely set at nought at the behest of a superior group. We ought to know that societies are as fallible as the human beings who constitute them. The argument about where somebody's loyalty is really due still has to go both ways.[6] It is not headstrong to keep arguing in both directions to safeguard two sets of values.

The argument about the merits of the one and the many ought to be a truth-seeking discussion weighing alternative priorities, but an unfortunate slogan has encouraged scornful partisanship. When Margaret Thatcher rashly said that there is 'no such thing as society', she was immediately deemed to have given voice to the worst sort of individualism, selfish and uncaring. It would have been less misleading had she said, 'There is no such *person* as Society'. Of course the communities to which people belong are significant entities, morally important, needing attention, deserving loyalty. 'Society' itself is still not a living conscious person, whose rights are to be upheld against other persons. One should more charitably suppose her to have meant, that if there are to be fears and wishes, pains and pleasures, sorrows and joys, it must be particular people not personified groups who worry and hope and who feel distressed or glad. That statement would have offered no encouragement to egotistical individuals to belittle their common life and hold themselves aloof from it. People's joining together in groups and living in human society is a most essential aspect of their moral existence; but the reason why groups matter and deserve loyalty is that they are made up of people.

As an analogy for the twin dangers, the tyrannical individual on the one hand and the group swallowing people up on the other, I may think of Scylla the swooping monster and Charybdis the gobbling whirlpool, the ancient alterna-

[5]   See above, p. 71.
[6]   ibid.

tive threats to travellers through the Straits of Messina. It is risky to navigate the ethical channel with perils on either side, at the mercy of the self-centred egoist and the oppressive collective. A zigzag course is necessary for avoiding both these unacceptable extremes. The hazard on the one hand is the egoism which separates each individual person from all the others as an disconnected being. The threat on the other hand is totalitarianism, which sacrifices individuals to their societies. The conflicts between these opposing dangers take everyday ethical shape. More or less independent people defend their own identity more or less strongly against more or less greedy groups.

To take up the particular problem — which Christians at least need to face in its own right — of how to relate the one and the many in the Christian church, a parochial matter indeed, can illuminate the wider enquiry about what it means to be *someone*. Understanding how much individuals matter, how they can go astray and what their unity means is especially important when the context is near home and ordinary. The prosaic concerns of church life supply examples which are all the more pertinent for being commonplace.[7] Everyday small-scale controversies, perennial rather than particularly topical, have general relevance, just because the people stuck in these difficulties are generally not heroes and villains but well-intentioned and doing their best. The transcendent claims of the Christian church, as they bear upon its more and less docile members, give rise to hard questions about fitting variegated individuals into this supernatural community which matters so much.

Though the presenting problems are ordinary, even petty, the claims made by this group are not petty. Is every Christian supposed to keep trying to make converts, in season and out of season, when the message conveyed to the people outside will most likely be that believers are a little mad? Would a young mother glorify God by frequenting church services, giving her family and her neighbours the impression that she finds this ploy of hers more important

[7]   This chapter is partly based on older work. See Oppenheimer (1970; 1988a; 1991).

than playing with her children? Piety is an ambivalent virtue. The very triviality of some of the rules religious people feel compelled to obey constitutes a problem which indeed is not trivial. It is serious that someone's deep concerns can come to look so shallow.

Some people who are far from being selfish individualists instinctively look upon their local church as an alarming Charybdis. They feel as if they are being put under unfair pressure to plunge into this whirlpool and identify themselves with this busy society which is trying to govern their lives. Here is a conspicuous practical illustration of the difficulty and desirability of balancing the one and the many. The literally parochial problems call attention to more basic moral arguments about the proper status of *I*, *they* and *we* and how their conflicting claims are to be responsibly weighed.

When the Gospel proclamation 'repent and believe' is interpreted as 'be committed, join our organization, do things our way', the noble idea of commitment is reduced to a caricature of itself, a commitment maybe to singing choruses and serving coffee. Fitting in with the particular style and using the particular terminology which the members of a church happen to find congenial can take on a surprising importance for a body of people who long ago began by turning the world upside down.[8] A would-be Christian might be brave enough to show a martyr's courage, but still hold back from enlisting in the body of believers, if that demands learning to speak an unnatural language and engaging in behaviour which feels insincere.

When the church came into being as the Body of Christ, of course the members of the body recognized its claims as their supreme concern. When followers of Christ two millennia later set about giving their church today the same kind of clear priority, are these enthusiasts more Christian than the ones who remain aware of multiple moral demands pressing strongly upon them? People cannot believe that appeals on behalf of the church must always

---

[8]   *Acts* 17.6.

take priority over secular good causes. Even less can they believe that they ought to count their own family doings as unimportant in God's eyes compared with the concerns of the parish. When it dawns upon them that the demands which are likely to be made upon them really are less important than the human claims of their daily lives, they do not feel equal to arguing. They quietly opt out and shed the wider loyalty for their narrower one. The one and the many lose touch with one another's points of view.

The pastoral problems about laying down the law or letting be, bearing witness or standing by patiently, allowing people to join in or to opt out, put in question moral assumptions about the nature of a person and about what it means to be a person in relationship with other persons. How highly ought the claims of 'someone' to be rated, when 'someone' is one person who needs to find a place among others? What ethical weight has one individual who is supposed to be bonded with other individuals in a purposeful group? If the group is a 'good cause', do its claims override other kinds of duty? Should appeals for everybody to enrol be received with caution as a threatening move to submerge people indiscriminately in the group identity? Because it is salvation which this group is offering, have other claims any weight at all?

For the people who are faced by questions like these, Christian faith does not solve their problems but even makes them harder. Of course membership of the Body of Christ must be a kind of membership which unites individuals more decisively than joining a bridge club. The members of Christ are not just his willing associates who pay their subscriptions, but are meant to be the human hands and feet which he uses now to act in the world. To ask how on earth they are to apply this conviction in practice forces them to confront the ambivalence of individualism.

The answer must be to discover the meaning of *fellowship*; but first this is really the problem. People declaring a message which means a lot to them are inclined to use large words, apparently taking it for granted that everyone will understand and be suitably inspired. When jargon begins to take over, it is worth making the effort to bring the terminology back to life by giving fresh attention to the meanings of words and considering what one is really trying to say.

Encouraged by their scriptures, Christians get a warm glow from the idea of fellowship. In the New Testament there recurs the Greek word *koinonia*, which signifies both 'fellowship' and 'communion'.[9] This keyword, whose primary meaning is 'partnership', opens up a complex of fundamental Christian convictions about sharing, having in common and participating. The first followers of Christ experienced the *fellowship* of the Holy Spirit as the foundation of their *community*. When Christians *share* bread and wine in Holy *Communion* they become one body with the Lord and with one another. They can enliven their faith by considering the meanings and connections of these ideas which all go back to *koinonia*.

Christians who tell one another to 'make Christian fellowship real' risk shrinking the everyday language of faith into a cliché. They almost but not quite succeed in passing on how the biblical teaching about belonging to the Body of Christ does indeed already apply to their church membership. 'Come and enjoy the fellowship and the most delicious soup', recommended a parish news-sheet with a happy touch of self-mockery. Christians know perfectly well that the fellowship of the Holy Spirit cannot be scheduled to appear at polite and pleasant events in churches, parish halls and sitting rooms.[10] Their real unity transcends superficial sociability. Yet the loyal community may not notice how their specialized vocabulary appears to ignore the other authentic kinds of loving commitment belonging to people's closest relationships, which are going on outside.

If the group which matters so much looks like a clique, it will be daunting rather than welcoming to enquirers, disheartening and even diminishing to a good many insiders as well.[11] Instead of 'The hungry sheep look up and are not

---

[9]   See e.g. *1 Corinthians* 1.9; *Philippians* 3.10.

[10] See, for example, article on 'Fellowship' in Atkinson & Field (1995).

[11] See Oppenheimer (1970), pp. 72f, 76; cf the last paragraph of the article on 'Fellowship', to which one can say 'Hear, hear.'

fed', Ronald Knox proposed, 'The sheep look fed up and are not hungry.'[12] When Christians feel themselves permitted and even obliged to give pious preoccupations an artificial moral priority, they belittle both the Christian community itself and the fellowship they hope to find there. The community of faith which is supposed to nourish them becomes an impediment, the penny near the eye blotting out the sun of Christian charity.

The damage is bound to be noticed by enquirers who want to know whether the 'good news' really is any good. Outsiders who find themselves either pressed to come in, on daunting conditions, or coldly excluded as unworthy, will see the behaviour of faithful people as an especially clear example of getting the balance of 'I' and 'we' wrong. They will reject the idolatry of the prized community, in which 'someone' is stifled, and the upshot will be to promote the converse idolatry of the prized individual, whose attitude is, 'I care for nobody, no not I, and nobody cares for me.'

People who have confidence that 'we' are the ones who know the Truth conclude that the ones who have different practical priorities must be at fault. People who hold back from church-belonging exemplify selfish individualism and their affectionate, even profound, relations with one another cannot be fully authentic in God's eyes. Someone who is not a 'joiner' is to be blamed as certainly lukewarm, probably unthinking and possibly lacking in ethical integrity.

The moral over-confidence which haunts some kinds of Christianity in every generation is less surprising if it is identified as, precisely, Pharisaical.[13] The Pharisees were the best and most devoted believers of their day, but the corruption of the best is the worst. 'Lilies that fester smell far worse than weeds.'[14] The censoriousness which is a characteristic failing of virtuous people often arises simply from mistaken loyalty or a lack of imagination, but what it looks

---

[12] See Oppenheimer (1988a), pp. 67–68.

[13] ibid.

[14] Shakespeare, *Sonnet* 94.

like from outside is plain hard-heartedness, making void the word of God by our tradition.[15]

That judgment in turn is not fair. As usual, there are contrary ways of seeing the case. The contented members of groups, the gathered two or three who enjoy one another's company and distance themselves from the lazy and worldly outsiders, may not deserve to have reverse blame heaped upon them for being exclusive, when more often they are understandably diffident. Because they realize how counter-productive evangelistic zeal can be, they feel that the task of preaching the Gospel to these reluctant joiners is not for them.

What judgmental Pharisaism lacks is respect for persons in their variety. Can the devoted members of the Body of Christ try to comprehend why *someone* may not want to conform and come with them? There are many other reasons for lack of commitment beside lukewarmness and most of them are honourable.[16] Outgoing enthusiasts persistently underestimate ordinary human shyness, which shrinks from showing off, and reserve, which has regard for people's privacy and does not expect to share everything with everybody. Self-consciousness is not always self-centredness. Extroverts appear to have little idea of the tormented embarrassment which overcomes many decent and by no means irreligious people at the idea of being greeted with a warm hug or asked whether they pray. Contented insiders need more developed sensitivity for beginning to understand what these unforthcoming strangers, half in, half out, really want.

It may be that what the outsiders want is not so different from what the insiders want. If the authorized group is not succeeding in providing the nourishment human beings require, they will have to provide it for themselves. Whether people are conventionally devout or not, they have diverse needs which go beyond prosaic everyday existence. Pious terminology may repel them, but it still matters to them to bless marriages and births, to mark the

[15] *Matthew* 15.6.
[16] See Oppenheimer (1970), p. 75.

milestones of growing older, to mourn and give thanks for their dead, to cheer themselves up in the middle of winter, to link themselves somehow to the world of nature and the fruitfulness of the earth, and to celebrate their solemn public occasions.[17] The shorthand for all this is 'folk religion'.

People who disapprove of other people's folk religion may not comprehend that when the ones outside the sheepfold come and ask for rituals to encourage and fortify them they are as sincere as the orthodox ones inside. Human beings are physical creatures and need physical ways of keeping in touch.[18] English folk religion sits loose to fervent commitment but does not sit loose to outward and visible signs for conveying inward meaning.

In other words, folk religion is sacramental, even characteristically so. Christmas Day is celebrated outside church with all manner of effective traditional rituals: greetings and visits, decorations, presents and feasting. If insiders can stop disdaining this enjoyment as if it were nothing but consumerism, and be ready to appreciate it as goodwill, it may turn out that ordinary human hospitality is capable of entertaining angels unawares.[19] Inasmuch as people make one another welcome, they may be opening their doors to Emmanuel, God with us.[20] One might imagine the Second Coming happening at Christmas time. If the Lord suddenly appeared in glory among the worldly people decorating their trees and stuffing their turkeys, austere Pharisaical churchgoers might still see only 'a gluttonous man and a winebibber, a friend of publicans and sinners'.[21]

If the members of the in-group could be more appreciative of authentic fellowship among the ones outside, they could be less scornful about the uncommitted and less inclined to make unfriendly conditions for including them. The insiders could stop being so possessive over sharing their prized common life with newcomers who turn out to

---

[17] See Oppenheimer (1988a, pp. 75–76; 1991, pp. 4f).
[18] See above, p. 20.
[19] Hebrews 13.2, referring to *Genesis* 18.1–10.
[20] *Matthew* 25.40.
[21] *Matthew* 11.19 / *Luke* 7.34.

want a part in it. There are signs that this is happening, especially some recent changes in the rules so that more couples can be welcomed to church for their weddings. Instead of making outsiders fight sad battles for access to their means of grace, Christians can claim plenty of biblical warrant for offering happy hospitality to people who have failed to qualify as members. It was especially characteristic of their Lord to work at the fuzzy edges of institutional religion.[22]

Consideration of the ethics of belonging suggests how intimidating both the exclusive group looking inwards and the grasping group looking outwards may be. To stop worrying about the people on the edge and leave them out in the cold is not a Christian option. In the Christian church, of all places, the claims of the individual and the group must be reconciled. Christianity would be a non-starter if it could only pose the problems without beginning to answer them. On the one hand, the Body of Christ ought to learn to be a community taking care of individuals, not a collective imposing upon them. On the other hand, individuals ought to stop allowing 'we' to disintegrate into 'I + I + I'. Defeatism is not in order. Conflict between the one and the many is by no means the whole story. At the best, individuals are finding themselves nourished and encouraged by their belonging and communities are coming to life from the individual variety of their members.

What makes human beings so selective in their priorities and so unresponsive to the claims of the many is not always human selfishness so much as human finiteness. Most people manage to give their full attention only to a small number of individuals, with the rest of humanity there in the background. The demands of the communities which claim one's loyalty are the demands of persons, which have to be weighed against the valid claims of other persons. Christians are finite too and cannot justify themselves by spreading themselves too thin.

An individual who is daunted by the relentless claims of church membership might try not to look upon the Chris-

---

[22] e.g. *Matthew* 8.3; 9.20ff; 18.13f; *Mark* 2.15–19; *Luke* 7.37ff; 13.14; *John* 4.9.

tian church as a domineering *collective* requiring obedience, but to see instead a *collection* of people, a multitude, who need one another. Every one in this crowd is someone; and even though nobody can begin to meet all their needs, none of them can be deemed not to count. Christians have to keep asking, 'Who is my neighbour?'[23] and the answer is not general but specific. My neighbour is the one who is there, who is nearby, who may turn out to be anybody, who may need to be sought out, but who logically cannot be everybody since I am a finite somebody.

The reason for someone to belong to the church emerges more compellingly, if the fallible local human organization is not presented as an end in itself making claims upon its members, but offered as a means to an end, indeed a means of grace, available for its members. A church community is not there for its own sake but to keep people to keep in touch with their God and with one another; and to nourish and uphold them in their own diverse callings. The nourishment is not merely metaphorical. The Eucharist is a sacrament of nourishment, provided for feeding lives.[24] Physical bread represents spiritual sustenance. Martin Luther urged anyone in despair to 'go joyfully to the Sacrament ... and seek help from the entire company of the spiritual body...'[25]

The characteristic agreeable happenings which members like to arrange, with hymn sheets and coffee cups, can be allowed to fall cheerfully into place,[26] rather than taking an artificial priority as if sociability were the heart of Christian commitment. The 'fellowship' which looked alarming is not out of reach. Its elusiveness, when people think they can control it, is like the elusiveness of happiness or originality. Made into a direct aim, fellowship seems frustratingly self-defeating. Like happiness or originality, fellowship is able to appear spontaneously when people give unselfconscious attention to the specific concerns which they find laid upon them.

---

[23] *Luke* 10.29.
[24] See Oppenheimer (1988a, 75f; 1991, p. 2).
[25] Luther 'On the blessed Sacrament', quoted in Rupp (1953).
[26] See Oppenheimer (1970), pp. 77–78.

The upshot of this discussion of Christian community ought not to be surprising. Communication with other people is an essential key for understanding the nature and needs of human beings.[27] The alternative to selfish individuals, ignoring or excluding the outer world, need not be groups trying to gobble their members up. Rather than saying aggressively, 'Your lives belong to us,' or grudgingly, 'Better late than never', the people who belong already can say invitingly, 'How lovely to see you. Do come in: we have something to show you'. The best corrective to possessive versions of 'fellowship' is an ethic of welcome.

When Christians feel tempted to limit the invitation to well-behaved conformists, they could look outside their own tradition to the teaching of Mevlana, the founder of the whirling dervishes:

> Come, come, whoever or whatever you may be, come,
> Infidel, heathen, fire worshipper, idolater, come.
> Though you have broken your penitence a hundred times,
> Ours is not the portal of despair and misery, come.[28]

Further reading

Atkinson, J.D. and D.H. Field, ed. (1995) *New dictionary of Christian ethics and pastoral theology.* InterVarsity Press: 'Fellowship', pp. 379–380.

Oppenheimer, Helen (1970) 'Head and members' in *The sacred ministry* ed. G.R. Dunstan.

Oppenheimer, Helen (1988a) 'Making God findable' in *The parish church*, ed. Giles Ecclestone. The Grubb Institute.

Oppenheimer, Helen (1991) 'Belonging and the individual', *TRUST*, a newsletter of SCM Press Trust No.5.

---

[27] See above, pp. 14–16.
[28] English translation on his tomb at Konya in Western Turkey; see Oppenheimer (1988a), p. 68.

Chapter 10

Pronouns and Names

Richard loves Richard: that is, I am I.

King Richard III, V. iii. 83

People mind about themselves and self-love is even part of what it means to be a person, but self-love is not the whole story either in theory or in practice. Conflicts between the claims of the *one* and the claims of the *many* belong in the context of a large cluster of debatable interconnected contrasts. Human beings need to find out how to relate self and others; I and we; we and they; private and public; domestic and communal; friends, neighbours and strangers; personal and impersonal. There are plenty of ethical, social and political arguments going on, amicably or otherwise and lucidly or otherwise, about which of these categories matter most. People need one another's help in identifying their assumptions and getting their priorities right, trying to do justice to variegated and sometimes contrary points of view.

At least I must keep hold of the assurance that I am not an inaccessible isolated 'self'. I must not slip into the notion that it is an extraordinary achievement to get in touch with the other people who are part of my life. Communication is indeed fundamental to personal life.[1] Individuals generally realize that they really are not alone nor self-sufficient; and find themselves emotionally and morally bound to one another. When I understand that I am part of *us*, my relationships with other people come to life and they will allow me to matter along with them.

---

[1]   See above, pp. 14–16, 103.

If our conversations are to be fruitful, a watchful eye needs to be kept on the way 'we' loses its force when easy-going people wrap themselves in it like a comfortable blanket. It is tempting to say, or tacitly assume, 'We all understand what that means,' 'We all know that's wrong,' or 'We never take any notice of that.' Before letting oneself be routinely included, it is as well to unwrap the implicit arguments and keep asking, 'Who are "we" in *this* context?'[2]Am I willing to identify myself like this and to be joined with these particular others in making statements which are supposed to be obviously true? Or am I being gathered unthinkingly into a collective where I do not really belong, which is easy to enter but hard to escape? Am I slipping into disloyalty to the people with whom I really do belong? Sometimes the time comes to stand back from the group where I feel at home and look again at some of the assumptions which *we* are taking for granted, criticizing them candidly, not treacherously?

It may be adequate to feed into the conversation, 'Oh, but surely...' Sometimes the way a particular discussion is going obliges me to say more strongly, 'We mustn't assume this' or 'I don't think we ought to do that'; and then I need to make it clear that by 'we' I do mean myself and the people I am addressing at that very moment. If I mean not 'we' but 'you', then that is what I have to say: and all the more so if what I really mean is 'they'. Sometimes my duty is to say firmly, 'Stop!' The most telling prophets are the ones who find themselves bound to speak up bluntly about a recognizable harm being done here and now, not the preachers who keep confessing in general terms that 'we' are greedy and selfish, oppressing our neighbours, ruining the planet. True prophecy, insisted G. R. Dunstan, is concerned with specific wrongs. It is not 'a general recital of the sins and sicknesses of society, before a congregation which, in all probability, is only in a limited and corporate sense a party

---

[2]   See Oppenheimer (1983), pp. 9–10.

to them, and with no specific action possible or invited, and no specific remedy foreseeable or foreseen.'[3]

We, the first person plural, is not the only pronoun which places human beings together in an ethical world. To consider some of the ramifications of our ordinary repertoire of pronouns is a good way of exploring the ethics of our dealings with one another. I am not always standing side by side with other people nor bravely shoulder to shoulder, all of *us* looking outwards to watch *them* over there. I turn to look towards somebody else nearby, first person *I* to second person *you,* and we greet one another face to face with greater or less formality and with less or greater affection.

Martin Buber taught religious thinkers of an older generation to concentrate on the way people relate to each other one-to-one as *I and thou,* by taking heed of the second person singular.[4] He contrasted the warm 'mutual and reciprocal' relationships of persons with the merely 'utilitarian or objective relationships' which are suitable for things.[5] People of goodwill accordingly learned to devalue the impersonal third-person 'I-It' which deals with objects, in favour of 'I-Thou' which has regard to live people.

The permanent worth of Buber's contrast of Thou with It has been his emphasis on the moral significance of persons and their dealings with other persons. Although the English language no longer uses 'thou' in everyday speech, the distinction between the personal and the impersonal is as valid in English as in German and matters as much as ever. People are not to be looked upon as if they were things. This approach to ethics is based on minding and mattering. Because people are alive they mind, and because they mind they matter.[6] Buber's contrast of the personal Thou and the impersonal It made it impossible to overlook the moral importance of conscious awareness,[7] philosophically

---

[3]   Dunstan (1962).
[4]   Buber (1923/1937).
[5]   *Chambers biographical dictionary* (1990), p. 222.
[6]   See above, pp. 8, 35; Oppenheimer (1995/2003).
[7]   See above, Chapter 1.

puzzling though it is to see how consciousness fits into the world of science.

Yet still Buber's particular version of personalism is not a complete corrective to the human tendency to treat other people as things. Relationships are more varied than just the two categories of warmly personal, on the one hand, or aloof and uncaring, on the other. To suppose that whenever we cannot or will not say 'I–Thou' there remains only the impersonal 'I–It' is even counterproductive, because it unfairly dismisses whole areas of our lives. The familiar interactions which Buber's followers value as 'I–Thou rela-tionships' are not the only dealings between people which are morally valid. It is not only with their nearest and dear-est that people have real face-to-face communications. They can recognize the significance of all the other people among whom they find themselves, by making full use of the other personal pronouns *you*, *he* and *she*. Distant acquaintances and strangers, as well as the individuals one knows best and cares about most, can and should be regarded and addressed as persons, not managed as things.

Indeed persons may be better honoured when a sharp line is not drawn between 'I–Thou' and 'I–It' as two totally different attitudes. Instead of setting up this absolute differ-ence between personal and impersonal communication, so that all our interactions have to be one *or* the other, there is something to be said for allowing the edges to be blurred. The notion of relationship is not all-or-nothing and we need not dismiss most of our everyday dealings with other human beings as merely I–It, just because they cannot all be I–Thou. I may acknowledge the girl at the supermarket counter as a person by saying 'Good afternoon' to her and making a comment on the weather. Even if there is a long queue and I simply enter my PIN I am not thereby treating her as a thing. I can respect her personal dignity by organiz-ing my purchases for her to tot up on her machine, better than by expecting her to tell me about her joys and sorrows.

We have another personal pronoun as important as I, we, thou, you, he, she, and they. I do not ask anyone to tell *I* about anything. Children learn the word *me* quite readily

and say 'Tell me a story'. What they generally find more difficult to pick up is the complementary lesson, not to put 'me'
into service as a pronoun for all purposes. They are not to
say 'Me likes' but 'I like'; and this really is a hard lesson
because the imperative weightiness of 'me' is not easily put
aside. If someone asks 'Who's there?' I have still not learnt
to answer correctly, 'It's I'. Without hesitation, sophisticated and unsophisticated people alike reply ungrammatically, 'It's me'. 'Me' feels right for distinctly singling out my
own self. It identifies this person for the practical purposes
of living. To ask what it means to be *me* is a convenient peg
for hanging philosophical questions about what kind of
entity a person really is.

The notion of being *me* is closely connected with being
someone who can be called by name. When I say 'It's me' to
attract attention to myself, I present myself as a recognizable individual;[8] and other people need a proper name for
labelling which one I am. The pronoun 'me' itself is not,
after all, 'a name I call myself'.[9] The *name* of the governess
teaching her charges to sing 'Doh re mi' was not 'me' but
'Maria'. Someone who *is* 'me' is someone who *has* a name.
We identify particular other people by the characteristic
human act of calling them by their names, not always singling them out as 'you' or 'we', 'this one' or 'those', but saying 'John' or 'Jane'.

A recognizable individual who is named is promoted
from being merely 'it' and is allowed to be treated as a person, seriously or sometimes fancifully. To speak to some
body by name is to speak to somebody. Preachers put much
emphasis on the moment in the Fourth Gospel[10] when the
stranger whom Mary Magdalen had taken for the gardener
greets her by name and she recognizes that this is no
stranger but the risen Lord. A name indeed is more than a
convenient label. The ways people use names are laden
with ethical significance.

---

[8] See above, p. 44–45; also Oppenheimer (2006), chapter 4 'Recognizing'
     e.g. pp. 54, 56.
[9] In *The sound of music* by Rodgers & Hammerstein.
[10] *John* 20.16.

My name is my very own and just because it is mine it is available as a means of communication for other people to use when they want to get in touch with me. If I were anonymous I should be hard to find. No wonder Alice in Looking-Glass Land was disconcerted to find herself in the wood where she had lost her name.[11] The names people are given by their parents before they are old enough to have any say in the matter become, whether they like it or not, the recognized carriers of their identities. To change one's name is quite drastic.

Of course things as well as people are conveniently identified by being given proper names beginning with capital letters, but they are not expected to answer to their names. Places and buildings are located by name on maps without being personified. People launch ships by naming them ceremonially and sometimes they give more or less affectionate names to their cars, but they know that these are still things not persons. People do not talk to things, except in play, in poetry, by mistake, or in exasperation.

For children, the difference between people and objects is not yet clear-cut. They may begin by believing that their teddy bears are alive and go on to pretending that they are, suspending disbelief. By playing with their toys and loving their pets, treating dolls as conscious and dogs as people, they are not making a mistake. By engaging in the game of personifying they are learning about personal relationships, practising how to treat people. The inability of autistic children to play pretending games is an important feature of their difficulty in understanding other minds.[12]

Naming an animal is more serious than naming a toy. To treat an animal as a member of human society, as someone, is not just an educational game but is taken quite literally by children and adults, however much or little they suppose that the animal itself understands and whether or not they expect a response. People kept rabbits in wartime to supplement the meat ration, but they would exchange them with their friends' rabbits when the time came for eating them,

[11]   *Through the looking-glass*, chapter 3.
[12]   See above, p. 16, note 9.

because once one has entered into relationship with an animal one can hardly eat it for dinner.

Calling a cow Daisy or a puppy Fido is an intriguing intermediate stage on the way to treating other people as persons. We may give them their due or maybe we fail to give them their due. Human dealings with animals illustrate the complexity of what it means to honour the dignity of a person, because calling by name indicates that assumptions about relationships are being made, assumptions which give rise to ethical questions.

From prehistoric times *Homo sapiens* has taken possession of other creatures, not only by hunting them or farming them, but by adopting them as welcome members of human households. Often the process has worked both ways and it has been the animals who have adopted the human beings as protectors and providers. Animals and people have become part of each other's lives, almost friends. Their mutual affection is literal, not metaphorical. The domesticated animals who are at home among human beings truly belong inside not outside the human moral community.

Nowadays any relationship of dominance has become suspect and moral concern about the ways human beings exploit one another is being expanded into an analogous concern for exploited animals. Not only eating animals and not only training them to serve their owners are treated as unethical; but even loving them as pets has come under attack as an assault on their dignity. Taming has been compared with enslaving.[13] If someone cherishes a lapdog as if he were her child, enjoying his comic little ways and appreciating his devotion, how does that compare with the way kind well-meaning people have treated adult slaves like children, while basking in their loyalty? What should a personalist, someone who believes in personal value, have to say about either of these benevolently patronizing ways of relating to fellow creatures?

It is fair to take heed of defences of pet-keeping as well as indictments. Having first honestly admitted the extent of

[13] This is interestingly discussed by Brooks (1988); see Oppenheimer (2006), pp. 52–53.

human unkindness and the corruptibility of human self-confidence, one may reasonably add that the way some animals have evolved to live with human beings can be counted as a real advantage to the animals as well as the people. Not all upholders of animal liberation believe 'that domestication is of its nature tyrannical'.[14] S. R. L. Clark for example insists on 'the primacy of the historically founded household and tribal group, a community of many ages, sexes and species...'[15]

Being domesticated is something fundamental that happened to some animal species long ago. They cannot be set free by anybody's decision now. Slaves are subjugated people, but dogs are not enslaved wolves. It would be an act of justice to set a slave free and a freed slave may thereupon flourish, but there is no procedure available for manumitting domestic animals to live their own lives after long service. The evolution of dogs from wild ancestors to their tame descendents cannot be reversed even by people who disapprove of it.[16]

The distinction between tame and wild is like, and also unlike, the distinction between bond and free. Nor is it the same as the distinction between educated and uneducated. Its complexity is worth considering, in order to open one's mind to how complicated the notion of a personal relationship can be. It is realistic and ethical to acknowledge and emphasize that wild creatures really are wild, not candidates for people to tame and train. The lion cannot lie down with the lamb in the world we know. Keats 'had a dove and the sweet dove died', pining for its life 'in the forest tree'.

Though people can study animals, protect and cherish them and learn to understand them, they cannot form communities with wild animals, whether or not they believe that animals have rights. Lynne Sharpe explained that this inability is not because a chimpanzee is too stupid, nor even because he is not a person. It has to be accepted that 'We

---

[14] Clark (1997), p. 111.
[15] ibid., p. 106.
[16] Lorenz (1966).

cannot trust him',[17] in the way we can trust a guide-dog or a ridden horse; and community depends upon trust.[18] Likewise, Vicki Hearne recognized the 'ultimate unworkability of living with chimpanzees'.[19] 'The wolf has wolvish social skills, but he has no human social skills, which is why we say that the wolf is a wild animal';[20] whereas, she says, the wolf regards a human being as a wild animal. Even though people taught sign-language to an ape and cherished the hope that she might go on to teach others, eventually Washoe had to be kept in a cage, not liberated.[21]

The line can sometimes be blurred. There are pleasing tales of saints who have made friends with fierce creatures, from austere St Jerome with his lion for company in the desert; to St Francis looking on the wolf of Gubbio as his brother; or Androcles, about to be martyred in the arena, who was fortunate enough to encounter a lion from whose foot he had benevolently removed a thorn. Whatever positive or negative part one might try to assign to animal rights in these stories, their message is not that the animals are there for our sake, raw material for pethood. People cannot get to know wild animals unless they first honour their strangeness. To recognize them as creatures of God in their own right is an attitude befitting a saint.

Calling other creatures by name is an indication of what people think about those creatures' ethical status. Jane Goodall, the student of chimpanzees in the wild, gave names to her subjects, though she felt that this anthropomorphism needed defence.[22] She was neither taming the chimpanzees nor expecting to join their society. She was appreciating the convenience of distinguishing them from one another; and surely also expressing the respect implied by acknowledging a fellow creature as an individual. Without falling into sentimentally, she was rejecting the harsh scientific attitude which treats the conscious subjects of

---

[17] Sharpe (2005), p. 108; see above, pp. 73ff.
[18] Sharpe (2005), pp. 106–109.
[19] Hearne (1986), p. 32.
[20] ibid. pp. 22–23.
[21] ibid. p. 107.
[22] Goodall (1988), pp. 31–32.

research as objects, denying rather than affirming their particular dignity by identifying them only by numbers.

Calling people by name indicates some kind of acknowledgment, but acknowledgment is not always respectful. Naming can be the kind of familiarity which is not deferential nor welcoming but impertinent. There has always been a practical ethical problem for people who hope to progress from one form of greeting to another. In more formal societies, the question would arise for new acquaintances whether the time had come to drop 'Miss Brown' and say 'Anne'. Today nurses and carers wonder, or should wonder, whether this particular elderly patient is missing the warmth of being greeted as Tom or Mary, or alternatively will freeze with awkwardness when this brash young person fails to begin with Mr or Mrs Smith. For some people, nicknames are a minefield of embarrassment. The presumption of the instant first name and the condescension of the childish pet name are not brutal like the insolence of a prison guard who reduces people to numbers, but may still be ways of failing to honour the dignity of persons.

To make free with somebody's name may be worse than ill-mannered: it may be a threatening invasion. One does not have to be a member of an indigenous tribe to feel alarmed at suddenly hearing one's own name bandied about indifferently. The conviction that names give power is engrained in human consciousness. In the Book of Revelation 'he that overcometh' is mysteriously promised a white stone with a new name written upon it, which no one knows except the one who receives it.[23] The belief that a hostile spirit can be exorcized or dominated if one can find out its name finds expression in folk tales such as the story of Rumpelstiltskin. The notion that naming is a bid for control cannot be dismissed as merely primitive.

This kind of power is spooky, and the idea of the uncanny is akin to the idea of the holy. In the second chapter of Genesis, it is God the Creator, who has called the creatures into existence, who gives Adam the authority to call them

[23] *Revelation* 2.17.

by name.[24] The converse of this authority for human beings to name the beasts is the characteristic Hebrew reluctance to name the Name of God, on pain of irreverence and even blasphemy. The awe revealed by such fear is more authentic than mere superstition.

To have a proper name is to be identifiable, for good or ill. For an individual to be given a name lays a foundation for recognizing that individual's ethical status. A step has been taken towards the outlook that this named person is not only findable but worth finding: morally important, maybe irreplaceable. The notions of *respect* and, beyond respect, of *wonder* begin to dawn. That an individual matters like this may be what people are trying to indicate when they say that here is somebody who has a soul.

There is a gradual progression here, not a contrast between 'soul' and 'no soul'. At the most elementary level, any conscious creature, however anonymous, is more than an insentient object. It can be said to have a point of view.[25] In proportion to its sensitivity, it has an authentic claim not to be hurt, but that does not make it irreplaceable. Its dying if painless need not be morally important. People who buy free-range eggs, refuse to eat pâté de foie gras and support charities promoting animal welfare do not all feel bound to reckon that meat-eating is murder.[26] Some vegetarians find it permissible to eat shellfish. Most people have little compunction about swatting flies and think it is even a duty to put an injured animal out of its misery.

The way persons are valued is different. Persons are individuals who go beyond consciousness to self-consciousness. They look before and after.[27] As well as the right of any person not to be hurt, people also have the right that we shall distinguish them from one another, on pain of being counted as insensitive. By contrast, bees in hives, deer in herds and even sheep in flocks are, to be candid, much of a muchness; though it is fair to consider that the Good

---

[24] *Genesis* 2.19; see Stackhouse (2007).
[25] See above, pp. 43–44.
[26] Oppenheimer (2006), chapter 1 'Only human'.
[27] *Hamlet*, IV. iv; see above, p. 3.

Shepherd knows his own sheep; and that Lynne Sharpe finds individuality in free-range chickens.[28] Konrad Lorenz suggested[29] that it is aggressive predatory species which have the need, and the capacity, to develop particular personal relationships, whereas the association of 'peaceable herd creatures' is naturally anonymous, companionable maybe but not cooperative.

It is part of the meaning of 'person' that if one is lost a substitute is not just as good. People are irreplaceable. They are individuals: but not units to be weighed or measured. One must not try to do sums with people, rating them in order of excellence, weighing a daughter against a son, counting two acquaintances as equivalent to one friend, giving a doctor more or fewer marks than a farmer, balancing somebody's sense of humour against somebody else's dependability. Calculating people's value is like doing arithmetic with an abacus made of quicksilver. Some people rightly matter much more to me than others, but that is because of their places in my life, not their quanti fiable worth. We may say simply that people are all equal, but that is still too mathematical. People are incommensurable.

Deciding what particular recognizable beings are to count as individual persons seem, as usual, to be a matter of more or less rather than an absolute difference of kind. Humankind appear to exemplify the fullest personhood we know. It appears that the main criterion for being a person is to have enough distinctiveness to be recognizable to somebody.

People need names for keeping in touch with other people.[30] A solipsist, a 'lone-self-ist' would not need to use a name, because if solipsism were true the solitary person would have to live without any other people and face all alone whatever experiences might occur. Such a solitary self could manage with no name but with only the pronoun *I*: except that he, or for that matter she, could hardly manage at all. Personal life belongs in a public world. Even prison-

---

[28] Sharpe (2005), pp. 35–36.
[29] Lorenz (1966), p. 186.
[30] See above, p. 44–45.

ers kept in solitary confinement have been imprisoned by somebody, who still has to give them food to keep them alive. Robinson Crusoe did not start life on his island but had a history with other people in it. Everyone arrived in the world as a baby and had an upbringing of some sort. Being a person entails some kind of dependence on other persons, not only for leading a happy life but for leading any kind of life. That is not something which just happens to be true and which might have been otherwise. It is part of the ordinary meaning of 'person'.

It is intellectually and practically appropriate to reaffirm robustly that solipsism will not do.[31] There is a given concept of a person as a recognizable being, who cannot be coherently imagined as a lone individual wholly apart from the world of people and out of all relationship with any others. 'The self' as a solitary independent thinker is an artificial notion which could not carry the full ethical weight of what personal identity means.

Real people who are not enticed by solipsism, nor cut off from human society by distressing circumstances, do not think of themselves as self-sufficient. Tender loving care, 't.l.c.' for short, is something human offspring need in order to thrive and grow up as persons. There are stories of children such as the 'wild boy' of Aveyron,[32] who have somehow been removed from human company and have survived and matured on their own; and these are generally unhappy stories. Feral children develop as wild creatures. They do not turn out to be people like ourselves who need only to be taught our language and our ways to be included in our society. Kipling's Mowgli is an attractive fiction. Human lives are sustained by other people and depend on both physical and emotional nourishment.

Further reading

Brooks, D.H.M. (1988) 'Dogs and slaves', *Proceedings of the Aristotelian Society*.
Buber, Martin (1923) *Ich und du* (English translation *I and thou* 1937).

---

[31] See above, pp. 14–15.
[32] See Brewer, *Dictionary of phrase and fable,* 15th edition, 1995, p. 1157.

Clark, S.R.L. (1997) *Animals and their moral standing.* Cambridge University Press.

Goodall, Jane (1988) *In the shadow of man,* revised edition. Phoenix paperback.

Hearne, Vicki (1986) *Adam's task.* Heinemann.

Lorenz, Konrad (1966) *On aggression* English edition, Methuen.

Oppenheimer, Helen (2006) *What a piece of work.* Imprint Academic.

Sharpe, Lynne (2005) *Creatures like us.* Imprint Academic.

II. DIVINITY

Chapter 11

Presence

> ... she thought she would try the plan, this time, of walking in the opposite direction.
>
> It succeeded beautifully. She had not been walking a minute before she found herself face to face with the Red Queen, and full in sight of the hill she had been so long aiming at.

Lewis Carroll, Through the looking glass, Chapter 2

Christian humanists can travel a long way with sceptical humanists. They can cooperate in treating humanity as valuable and exploring together the tautology that *everyone is somebody*. They should be equally willing to abandon the two old prejudices, dualism[1] which separates the valuable soul from the poor mortal body, and atomism[2] which separates each person from all the others.

If Christians are still afraid to abandon soul-and-body dualism for fear that their valuable souls will disappear altogether, they may firmly reassure themselves that they can agree with unbelievers in looking on a person as a united whole. Believers can assuredly go on using the terminology of spirit[3] to express their faith that human life is more than physical material; but they are no more committed than sceptics to the notion of 'the ghost in the machine'.[4] A human being is not an insubstantial soul who just happens at the moment to inhabit a body, nor an angel and an animal awkwardly joined. Personal life, and in the end the

---

[1] See above, pp. 11f.
[2] See above, pp. 70f, 91.
[3] See above, pp. 33, 36.
[4] See above, p. 20.

eternal life which is the Christian hope, is a matter of whole embodied people inhabiting a physical world appropriate for their thriving.[5]

Still more readily, believers and unbelievers should agree to give up the assumption called atomism, which detaches each person from all the others as isolated units. The world we live in is one world. Christians and sceptics alike may take their stand on the practical and moral conviction that *we* is more fundamental than *I*. Communication is a central fact about people, even *the* central fact.[6] Objects can touch each other but people are able to be *in touch*. Their moral existence is based upon their capacity to live in relationships.

But of course Christians do have to part company with sceptics, not by affirming that each person is someone who matters to other people, but by asserting that there is, in fact, a supreme Someone over all. Christians see human life as belonging under the rule of a personal God, with whom they believe that human persons can communicate. They are committed to the belief that whatever they do they are always in the presence of God.

What spiritual presence may mean is not a problem for sceptics because they are content to stay with simple physical presence. If they use soul-language at all, they treat it as metaphorical. They do not expect to recognize God's personal presence in the world and they do not feel obliged to puzzle themselves about what kind of entity a spirit might be. Gladly or regretfully, sceptics inhabit a secular universe. When they want to understand what it is to be 'someone' they can ring the changes on *living body, human being, person, individual, self...*, and even on *soul* and *spirit* when they want to attend to deeper aspects of their lives;[7] but they need not tangle with a world beyond the range of science nor have any dealings with ghostly presences. Believers find themselves swimming in more turbulent waters.

---

[5] See above, p. 27; see Oppenheimer (1988); cf St Paul: *Romans* 8.23, *1 Corinthians* 15.44; *2 Corinthians* 5.1–3.

[6] See above, pp. 15ff.

[7] See above, pp. 8, 42f.

Belief in spiritual reality makes the straightforward physical notion of *being present* into a difficult notion. We understand from everyday experience what bodily presence
means, but people have not seemed to be talking nonsense
when they have enlarged the idea of being present beyond
the paradigm case of literal seeing and touching. Nowadays
technology has made one way of extending personal presence possible and ordinary. Human beings can interact
with one another, without being physically nearby, by
means of the seemingly magical telephone, 'far-speech',
and television, 'far-sight'. But long before these were
invented, people sometimes became aware of vivid experiences of personal communication which were not a matter
of material bodies face to face or side by side.

When people feel as if the spirits of the beloved dead are
watching over them, or that certain places are haunted by
ghosts, or that a force not their own is inspiring them, or
indeed as if devils are tempting them or that there is some
awesome Power to be propitiated, there are plenty of psychological explanations which can be produced, kindly or
scornfully, without recourse to the supernatural. And yet:
these tenacious notions about presence which is spiritual
without having to be bodily are not easily eradicated,
because they belong to complete systems of thought built
up over generations, too deeply rooted to dig up. When
people promise in sentimental or jocular fashion, 'I will be
with you in spirit', they are drawing on what feels like a
stock of real human experience.

Many human beings besides eccentrics and mystics have
used the language of spiritual presence to describe their
conviction that they could talk to God who is Spirit. A philosopher who had learnt from Wittgenstein might say, 'This
language-game is played.'[8] Children learn language by
being taught to join in different 'language-games', trying
them out and seeing what happens. Prophets who have
appeared to be quite sane have used religious language to
report in detail what God has said to them. They may be

[8]   Wittgenstein (1953), e.g. section 7.

mistaken but they are not simply daft or deceitful. They have lived and died by these experiences, which need to be judged by their fruits.[9]

It was all very well for the first Christian theologians, already confident of finding God the Creator present in the world, to plunge without hesitation into the metaphysical language about Holy Spirit and human spirits, not doubting that it would make sense. Their twenty-first century successors are obliged to be more cautious, because they have to do their thinking in a universe in which belief in Someone up there, an active ever-present God, no longer looks like the most natural and obvious explanation of the world they inhabit. Since Darwin the terms of reference have changed. Though the discovery of evolution has by no means undermined the wonder of the universe,[10] it has undermined the easy argument that the wonderful universe evidently needs a Creator, to account for the existence of such a variety of creatures. Once people grasp how animals, including human beings, could develop of their own accord, they may begin to feel that they get on better without worshipping a mighty Spirit who made and sustains this painful world but who is nowhere to be found when they cry out for help.

On the contrary, they may feel obliged *not* to indulge in such mystifying notions. They do not need to explain the universe as God's creation and it can look very much as if they ought not to try. Many sceptics feel, not just an intellectual relief at getting rid of the metaphysical problems about how God, who is pure Spirit, could impinge upon the physical world, but a moral relief at being allowed to declare honestly that they have failed to find God's presence. Where is God in this inoperable tumour or that tsunami? If as a Christian I mention some happening in my life which I believe is an example of God's grace, instances can quickly be provided of God's distressing absence from the lives of more

[9]   *Matthew* 7.16, 20.
[10]   See above, pp. 33–34.

deserving people.[11] It is callous to be staunchly stoical about other people's troubles, and surely more ethical to acknowledge God's elusiveness.

The presenting problem about how to understand spiritual presence has led straight into what looks like a wrecking difficulty about whether we ought to depend upon any such concept. The more I wonder about where to find God, the less I seem able to explain what 'finding God' could mean. Can I produce a good plain example to show somebody what I mean by God's particular response to my prayers?[12] Pushing on doggedly with confident slogans about Christian spiritual experience looks like offering as an answer what is really a large part of the problem. The best way to go on may be to step back.

Rather than taking for granted that of course faith finds God's grace manifest everywhere in creation, wherever we may look, it is more promising to ask whether or not Christian belief really needs this assurance and indeed to answer boldly that it does not. Instead Christians could take as a foundation the idea of a Creator who may not yet be 'all in all'.[13] They can begin by putting aside for the time being the idea of God as an ever-present but elusive Spirit, and they can use instead an image of their God as more like an individual Person, who may be found here or there. Theologians will be inclined to object that this reduced notion of God will never do and label it *deism*. Picturing God naively as Someone somewhere cannot be the whole story; but still a Christian kind of qualified deism may turn out to give faith a better start than free-range metaphysics.

Plain deism is indeed a meagre theology, which does persist in affirming that God is real, but refrains when it comes to the point from expecting God to appear in the physical world or to make any difference to the course of events.[14] A deist is somebody who asserts that the good God made the universe and then left it to its own devices, an idea which

[11]   cf. Oppenheimer (1991), p. 73.
[12]   Oppenheimer (1973).
[13]   *1 Corinthians* 15.28.
[14]   Oppenheimer (1973), p. 57.

evidently does not say enough for believers and still says too much for sceptical scientists who do not need that hypothesis. Christians have been glad to reject deism as a heresy, but they have been apt thereupon to lurch into a contrary assumption that God must be *omnipresent*, and that whatever happens in the world, however regrettable, God must have done it and God's will must be revealed there

When children ask, 'Where is God?' the standard answer is 'God is everywhere'. That is supposed to be encouraging, but it does not provide much help in finding God anywhere in particular. Faith can hardly find a foothold upon such a nebulous foundation: but maybe it is unnecessarily defeatist to suppose that it should. 'Everywhere' may even be a misleading start. It does not seem to lead is not towards Christian belief in the heavenly Father, who in the fullness of time sent his Son, but rather towards *pantheism*, which looks on the whole universe as divine, at the risk of losing God among all the things there are.

Christian are not obliged to imagine God's presence as evenly spread. 'Scripture knows no "Omnipresence"', said Rudolf Otto,[15] 'it knows only the God who is where He wills to be, and is not where He wills not to be'. It seems that sometimes God withdraws. When Christians find themselves experiencing in their lives not the presence but the absence of God, they need not feel bound to keep declaring indiscriminately that 'God is here' whatever the circumstances, endangering their faith and one another's. The Christian creeds make more precise and more encouraging announcements about God's real particular presence, which people troubled by intellectual doubt urgently need.

Confronted by their own or other people's devastation, Christians may honestly and loyally refuse to believe that 'God did this'. Faith in God is compatible with agnosticism and even scepticism about Providence. When dreadful events make people ask, in despair or compassion, 'Where is God?' they may allow themselves to realise, like Elijah, that 'the Lord was not in the earthquake', nor in the hurri-

---

[15]   Otto (1923), Appendix VIII p. 214; see Oppenheimer (1973), p. 194.

cane nor the fire.[16] They may even suggest, 'an enemy has done this.'[17] What matters is not that God is revealed everywhere but that God has been revealed somewhere.

Christian faith is based on Jewish monotheism, which is not afraid of making definite statements. The one Lord God created heaven and earth; made a covenant with Abraham; acted dramatically to rescue His chosen people from their slavery in Egypt; gave the law to Moses; and spoke by the prophets. This Deity was surely to be thought of as an individual Someone. In ancient Israel it was not a struggle to imagine God as a particular recognizable Person. Throughout their early history God's people were more troubled by rival gods than by puzzled thinkers wondering whether faith had any meaning. It was only the 'fool' who said in his heart that there was no God at all.[18]

What Christians have built on this heritage is the conviction that in the fullness of time the presence of the Lord God has been decisively revealed through one particular man, Jesus of Nazareth, whose followers came to recognize him as the unique Son of God. They recount that he was born of a woman and grew up as a human being who taught and acted in the name of his Father; that he was killed by his enemies; that he was raised by God; that he has defeated death; and that in all this he was the bodily manifestation of the love of God in action for the sake of human creatures. They can give some account of their evidence for accepting as fact this paradigm case of God's dealings with the travailing world. Their characteristic affirmations about how they have found God's presence abiding with them are founded upon this particular narrative. They offer a *crucial* answer to the cry that the Creator who gives no sign is a sham. More sophisticated theological assertions may follow as required.

There is no need to try desperately to identify God's providence in tragedies and calamities, since the primary place to find God is the coming of Christ. If Christians are told that God directs everything, and that unless they believe this

---

[16] *1 Kings* 19.11–12.
[17] *Matthew* 13. 26–8.
[18] *Psalm* 14.1.

they are merely deists,[19] they may indeed be willing to be called *incarnational* deists. They should be relieved to stop trying to locate God's activity indiscriminately in whatever happens.

Standard deism is a world-view as unsatisfactory as the pantheism which is its converse. Pantheism supposes that everything in the universe is God: deism supposes that God is aloof from everything in the universe. Christians on the contrary affirm that 'the Word was made flesh and dwelt among us'[20] at one definite time and place. They can therefore face the recurring challenge of God's elusiveness and proceed to develop a working faith, on the foundation of this special life where they believe God's presence has been found.

It is a more telling response to sceptical doubt to begin by saying, naively, that God has visited the creation than to rush into saying, obscurely, that God is omnipresent in the creation. God's presence with humanity is paradoxically recognized in an individual man who himself went through the common human experience of God's absence.[21] Provided that this narrative of disaster and vindication carries conviction, believers aware of the sufferings of the world, who are failing to find any sign of Providence, may concentrate the Christian creed into the central claim that wherever else God may or may not appear, 'God was in Christ'.[22]

This preliminary shrinkage consolidates the foundations of faith. Christians can stop expecting their God to keep making decisive divine interventions in the course of events, and then being upset because the world is not like that. They can sit loose to special providences in their own lives. They are allowed to be mystified about what God's presence in the world means, like cooks boiling kettles without studying physics.

Believers who identify the Incarnation of Christ as the needful decisive example of where to find God need not be

[19]   See Oppenheimer (1973), chapter 4 'What think ye of Christ?'.
[20]   *John* 1.14.
[21]   *Psalm* 22 & *Mark* 15.34.
[22]   *1 Corinthians* 5.19; see Bauckham (1997), p. 188.

perturbed to find that they have arrived at a kind of deism. They may find contemporary claims about divine grace too unconvincing to give their faith a firm foundation, and the ancient stories of God's dealings with Israel too remote, but they can be ready to fall back on a deistic idea of a God who made the world and mostly lets it be. The necessary condition for Christian belief is to say something positive about where they do recognize God's presence and build upon that. They can set about developing a full-scale Christian theology which is able to recognize frankly how far from divine the creation often appears for its inhabitants, since the God who made it has been one of those inhabitants and knows at first hand what it is like. They need not hold back nervously from historical study of earlier times, nor from scientific study of the natural world,[23] for fear that their faith may be defeated by the everyday recalcitrance of life.

This argument, as I tried to present it in 1973, that the personal God who often seems to be absent can be located as coming down to earth in one specific human life, was soon overtaken by the controversy about the '*myth* of God Incarnate'.[24] Radical theologians, who clearly still intended to be faithful Christians, found themselves unable to affirm in the old way that Jesus was literally God walking on the earth. They proceeded to adopt the word 'myth' for statements which are not plain fact but may none the less be profoundly true; but they should have realised that this was misleading, even tendentious, when the popular meaning of 'mythical' is simply 'imaginary'. Now that the dust has cleared, Christians have not found that their faith in Christ as *God with us* has evaporated into a superstitious illusion; but traditionalists are obliged now to state more cautiously and carefully why they do believe that 'God was in Christ'.

They will need to have a great deal to say, but two things in particular. First, before acquiescing in the assumption that if the Gospel can be described as 'myth' then it cannot be fact and must really be false, they should consider the different ways we use words to tell one another about the

[23] See above, pp. 33f.
[24] e.g. Hick (1977).

world. Our language constantly shifts between more and less literal. Metaphorical language can tell the truth. A poetic image is generally more than an attractive garnish. It can be the best way, or even the only way, of conveying real facts.

Figures of speech cannot always be translated without remainder into literal language; and not all true statements about the world can just as well be expressed in plain prose. It is not more truthful to say flatly, 'Her sufferings made her desperate' than to say more vividly 'Her sufferings broke her heart'. Nor is it more accurate to say 'He was fascinated and delighted' instead of 'He was enchanted'. When I *understand*, I am using a metaphor which is dead and I do not picture myself standing under anything; but when I find myself *enlightened* that metaphor is still alive, *illuminating* my thought. I may just as truly say that an idea has *dawned* upon me. People do not bend down to pick up the splinters of shattered dreams, nor train public watchdogs to come to heel, but when they experience dread they feel it weighing heavily upon them and when they are happy their hearts dance.[25]

If ordinary language is so crammed with imagery, all the more does religious language need to take imaginative shape to say what is beyond the reach of human intelligence. If we had to insist that figures of speech could be allowed only a decorative role, we would have to reject the grand possibility that there are more things in heaven and earth than human beings can say plainly. A God within easy reach of prosaic analysis would be an idol not a God, but believers may bow down with integrity before 'the high and lofty one who inhabits eternity.'[26] When we hope that our awareness may be capable of being stretched much further than its present limits, we need to grasp that stretching and grasping are already metaphors which we can hardly afford to forgo. Since ordinary life does not require us to speak only prose, attempts to make true statements about

---

[25] *Psalm* 28.8.
[26] *Isaiah* 17.15.

transcendent reality can be allowed to draw upon all the linguistic resources of humanity.

The second thing which believers must remember, when they explain how they need both literal and figurative language to convey what they mean, is that explaining what they mean is still not confirming that what they are trying to say is true. For establishing Christian faith, most of us must depend upon one another. Matthew Arnold on Dover Beach recommended human truth as itself providing a faith to live by.[27] People whose faith goes further than that, who find that they can hold on to the truth of the Christian Gospel, are still dependent upon the human truthfulness of the many other people who have handed on, through twenty centuries, what they themselves experienced.

When believers are required to give reason for the faith that is in them,[28] it is an appropriate response to explain how their own strong or weak consciousness of God's presence is buttressed by the inspiration and the honesty of the first Christians, communicated to following generations by the church they founded and the scriptures they wrote. Of course we need to be constantly reminded how different their world was from ours. It would nevertheless be defeatist to emphasize the foreignness of these fellow human beings so strongly as to discount their testimony, as if what they meant by good news had no bearing on twenty-first century hopes and fears.

'Since we are surrounded by so great a cloud of witnesses', urged the Epistle to the Hebrews, 'let us ... run with patience the race that is set before us, looking to Jesus the pioneer and perfecter of our faith'.[29] Twenty-one centuries later, Christians may find the image of a *chain* of witnesses more encouraging than a cloud. They may be still more encouraged by a recent book by Richard Bauckham,[30] who argues that the chain is shorter and stronger than critics have led them to suppose.

---

[27] See above, p. 38.
[28] *1 Peter* 3.15.
[29] *Hebrews* 12.1–2.
[30] Bauckham (2006).

As physicists appeal to their experiments, theologians appeal to human experience. They should not find it surprising that faith needs to be grounded in facts. Christians believe that they have come across facts which stubbornly indicate a realty which defeats description. For many reasons, which they must be willing to try to specify, they believe in God the Creator who came into the world as one particular human being. Their justification for affirming their faith is something like the justification of physicists, who find that their data compel them to make assertions which seem incomprehensible. The mind boggles but we can see where and how it begins to boggle and go carefully but boldly along with its boggling.

Further reading

Oppenheimer, Helen (1973) *Incarnation and immanence*. Hodder & Stoughton: Chapter 3 'The identifying of grace'.

Chapter 12

Someone Up There

I asked the sea, the deeps, the living creatures that creep, and they responded, 'We are not your God, look beyond us'... And with a great voice they cried out: 'He made us.'

St Augustine, *Confessions* X, vi. 9

Some Christians have the strenuous task of interpreting the message which has come down to them, in order to communicate responsibly to their own contemporaries how they understand the idea of a personal God, whose Spirit is present to human persons. To the insistent enquiries about where to find God, they can answer, 'God was in Christ';[1] but they cannot relax here for long.

The first followers of the Risen Christ found themselves speaking about him in two ways. They made plain assertions about Jesus as an individual man, who had lived a human life in their contemporary world; and also they made mysterious assertions about the Spirit of Christ, whose divine life his disciples could share. Christians cannot escape from questions about what *incarnation* can mean, what sense it makes to say that God lived a human life. How is this particular man different from other people? May we pray to him without falling into idolatry? Have Christians after all abandoned the prized monotheism of Abraham, Isaac and Jacob and taken up worshipping a human being? It could never be the whole story to leave God the Father Almighty aside and have faith only in the Lord Jesus.

These are the questions which led step by step to the doctrine of the Trinity. Putting their lively experience into

---

[1]   *1 Corinthians* 5.19; see above, p. 125.

words, Christian theologians came to describe the One God, whom the children of Israel had been worshipping all along, as a unity of three Persons: the heavenly Father, who made the heavens and the earth; Jesus Christ the Son, who entered into human life; and the Holy Spirit who pervades the whole creation. However abstruse all this became, it began as the stuff of everyday Christian living.[2]

The idea of God as threefold did not arrive as a human invention ingeniously devised to make Christian theology more sophisticated. People who believed in one God, who had come to find the particular presence of God in Jesus Christ, realised that they needed the formula of Father, Son and Spirit to express their new experience of God's dealings with them. In saying 'Jesus is Lord' they were not idolatrously worshipping another divinity, for 'the Godhead of the Father, of the Son, and of the Holy Ghost, is all one'.[3] They still reckoned themselves as loyal monotheists when they learned to pray *to* the Father, *through* the Son, *in* the Spirit; but their creed had to become more complicated.[4]

Christian faith still starts with the announcement made to God's people long before, 'Hear O Israel, the Lord our God is One Lord.'[5] The Gospel stands on this base. Whatever else believers may try to say about the life of the One God, they immediately proceed to apply to themselves the commandment which follows, 'and thou shalt love the Lord thy God'.[6] God is to be loved. Christians go on to develop their characteristic affirmation that God *is* love.[7] When they are asked how they know that this is true, they offer their particular account of how God the Son came down from heaven in order to enter into a particular human life and take part in the afflictions of human creatures. The historical narrative about Jesus Christ is not the whole Christian faith but the way in to the mystery of God the Holy Trinity.

---

[2]   See above, p. 9.
[3]   The 'Creed of St Athanasius' (*Book of Common Prayer*).
[4]   See Oppenheimer (1973), p. 204.
[5]   *Deuteronomy* 6.4.
[6]   *Deuteronomy* 6.5 / *Mark* 12.30 / *Matthew* 22.37 / *Luke* 10.27.
[7]   *1 John* 4.8.

The Christian creeds are certainly paradoxical. We do not all need to grasp their meaning, any more than we all need to master nuclear physics in order to handle the solid objects around us, but we have to grasp that something can be true and make a difference to our lives even if it is beyond our understanding. Theologians work at exploring the paradoxes for the sake of themselves and other people, hoping that the doctrines will turn out to be justified, in theory and in practice, by being found to illuminate the world we know.

The belief that God came to earth as a human being offers an answer both to theological questions, about how people can recognize God's presence, and to ethical questions, about how people can believe that God is good. Not all followers of Christ find these problems hard; but when they do, they should not be told, 'That's no business of yours: just have faith.' It still matters for believers today not merely to parrot the biblical statements but to begin to see their meaning. Because it mattered so much to the Christians who first handed on the Gospel to grasp who Jesus Christ was and is, Christian theology cannot be reserved for professional theologians.

Some people find it straightforward to believe that God made the world and looks after it, and they discover in their daily lives that God is with them. They can comfortably include both these ideas, God above us, and God alongside us, in the package of Christian faith. God over all is what God's *transcendence* means, and God invisibly present in all creation is God's *immanence*.

When people's confidence is wobbling, and God's invisibility simply looks like God's absence, then the particular Christian doctrine of God's *incarnation* comes alive: that God is recognizable in one individual human life. This assurance that God does not have to be findable everywhere in general because God is findable somewhere in particular is the most promising beginning for people who long for an example of God's positive presence. They can locate God specifically in the life, death and resurrection of Christ.[8]

---

[8]   See above, p. 124.

'God was in Christ' offers a paradigm case, a crucial example, of God's availability, which is fit to be a firm base for a more comprehensive creed. Once this is in place, it can support, all the better, a renewed readiness to find God anywhere in creation.[9] When Rudolf Otto boldly denied that God was always present everywhere,[10] he was a long way from being a deist whose God made the world long ago and now remains aloof. Otto went straight on to say that this God who is sometimes absent is also able to be 'closer than breathing' to us.[11] He was quoting Tennyson[12] but he was expressing a notion of God's nearness which would have been recognizable for St Paul.[13] The God of the Christian creeds is indeed within reach, not automatically but when God chooses to be within reach.

In thinking about God as both high above the world and present within it, it would be foolish to neglect the resources of earlier Anglican scholarship. Nearly a century ago, C.C.J. Webb took up the theme of God's dealings with humanity, and was especially concerned to ask whether Christians rightly think of God as *personal*.[14] His balanced arguments could still be an encouragement for further thinking.

Webb would not have been attracted to the plain notion of God as Someone.[15] His terms of reference were provided by the high-minded idealist philosophy of the early twentieth century, which spoke more readily about God as the Absolute than about God as Father; but he was far from being fixed in that mindset. Rather than lose touch with traditional Christian piety, in book after book he wrestled with what it means to apply the idea of personality to God, though he would not call God 'a person' like us.

It is worth picking up his old-fashioned arguments: not expecting to settle the question how to think about God, but

---

[9] See above, p. 33.
[10] See above, p. 123 and note 15 there.
[11] Otto (1923), Appendix VIII, p. 214.
[12] Tennyson 'The higher pantheism'.
[13] e.g. *Acts* 17.27–28.
[14] e.g. in his Gifford Lectures, Webb (1918–1919); see Oppenheimer (1973).
[15] See above, p. 122.

to feel the sting of the problem and to see why it matters. Does it make sense to say that God is both above and beyond the creation and also findable within it? It was of great concern to C. C. J. Webb to be able to speak about God in personal language. He would not imagine God as someone comfortably like ourselves, but it was especially important for him to affirm real mutual personal relations between oneself and God. 'Reciprocation' was a keyword. Faith cannot be satisfied by one-way acknowledgement of the holy but impassive Absolute who takes no interest in the creation and does not mind about people.

For all his loyalty to traditional Christian belief in a personal God who takes part in personal relationships, Webb did hold back from calling God 'a person' and explained why this would not do. He pointed out that the notion of 'the Personality of God' is not ancient but goes back no further than the eighteenth century. He insisted that if God were 'just another person standing side by side' with us, superior and powerful like the gods of ancient Greece, we should feel no religious encouragement but 'a sense of insecurity and outrage' at the idea of the innermost thoughts of our hearts being pried upon. The philosopher John McTaggart (1866–1925) expressed a similar uneasiness: 'But it can't be nice to believe in God, I should think. It would be horrible to think that there was anyone who was closer to one than one's friends.'[16]

It is not only philosophers who feel dissatisfied with the notion of a God too much like ourselves. When traditional churchgoers resist the current fashion for addressing God easily as 'You', just like anyone else we might meet, it may be this kind of discomfort which underlies their reaction. People who still want to retain the ancient form 'Thou' are not nostalgically stuck in olden times. Nor are they holding God at arm's length as a stranger: by no means. 'Thou' is closer than 'You'. They are trying to express in their worship their reverent recognition that the God to whom we

---

[16] In a letter quoted in Baillie (1934), p. 274; cf Oppenheimer (1973), p. 117.

are allowed to speak so familiarly is not an ordinary person just like us.

Rather than fall into describing God as merely a particular individual among others, C. C. J. Webb was prepared to run the contrary risk of seeming to encourage the lofty but hazy worldview of pantheism. He liked to quote a bad pun of Carlyle's: 'What if it be Pot-theism, so it be true?' He surely cannot be accused of being a pantheist if what pantheism means is thinking of God as some kind of impersonal force; and still less if pantheism suggests that the universe itself is God. His emphasis was on the notion of God's Spirit, 'animating the world and entering our inner life'.[17]

The heart of C.C.J. Webb's personalism, which makes it still relevant for Christian theology, was his orthodox belief in the Trinity. By affirming that God is Father, Son and Holy Spirit, he could avoid calling God '*a* Person' and affirm 'personality *in* God'. This is no mere debating point, like saying, 'No, there isn't a cat in this room: there are three.' The conviction that God is not a solitary Being is the foundation of the characteristically Christian moral assertion that 'God is love'. God has someone to love before God has a world of people. The ancient high-minded notion that the spiritual life is 'the flight of the alone to the Alone' is far from being a Christian idea.

If without us God would be solitary, God's love could only be egotistical. God would have to be occupied in simply loving God's own self. The Christian creeds affirm that God apart from creatures is already not alone. Relationships of love, built into God's own being, come before God's auspicious loving-kindness towards the beloved creatures which God's power in due course brought into existence. The two-way personal relations between human beings and God which Webb was so concerned to stress are based upon the theology of 'three Persons in one God'. This emphasis is what brings Webb's thinking about God and personality to life for Christian understanding today.

---

[17] Webb (1911), p. 222.

If God is indeed Three in One, it is even more true for God than for us that *we* is more basic than I.[18] The theology of the Father, the Son and the Holy Spirit is not just a sort of extra complication which the first Christians had a compulsion to tack on to a simple faith in the Lord Jesus. The dogma of the Trinity means more than a clever formula to allow believers to worship Jesus Christ and still call themselves monotheists. Reciprocal love is built into God's own nature all along, before God's love is revealed in creating and saving the universe. The doctrine of the Trinity is the mystery underlying the story of how God the Son came into the world, died and rose again.

Without the doctrine of the Trinity, the One God would need the creation in order to have anybody else to love. God would have to depend upon creatures for emotional satisfaction. If it is true that the One God of the Hebrews has turned out to be threefold, Christians can repudiate any idea that God depends upon loving relationships with human beings, like lonely old people whose life revolves around their beloved pets. God is self-sufficient and is not in need of anybody else. Creatures are, so to speak, extra. People are welcomed into the original eternal love of the Holy Trinity, not because God needs them but because God wants them for their own sakes. This is the encouraging meaning of the time-honoured austere doctrine that God is *impassible*: that God is infinitely stable and unshakable. There should be no menacing suggestion that God is *unfeeling*.[19] God's love for the world is voluntary, lively and magnanimous, and 'amazing grace' is no cliché but truly astounding.

The confident insistence that God is Love presupposes that it makes some kind of sense to think of God as Someone. Christians take this as given and for them the question has become, Is God three Someones?[20] The oddness of the grammar underlines the oddness of the idea. Does 'three Persons' mean 'three centres of consciousness', as it would

[18] See above, pp. 16, 66.
[19] See below, p. 177–78.
[20] Oppenheimer (1973), p. 205.

if we were talking about human persons? Faithful people can hardly help wondering after all whether they are fighting a losing battle against plain nonsense. As usual, the possibility of belief in God depends upon the possibility of trusting the testimony of other people.[21]

Christians who are not mystics have to decide whether the reliability of the witnesses, from the first century to the present day, who have reported their decisive experience of this mysterious God is strong enough to stand up against the reliability of such sophisticated assailants as Professor Dawkins. Believers need not expect to be provided with knock-down proofs in this life. Nor need they expect to be able to imagine what it would be like to be God. What they can say is, 'Let's try this and see how we get on.' Their responsible hope is that by entering into the tradition they will come, as many others have done, to enter into some awareness of being wanted children of God.

Instead of relentlessly pressing the question whether three Persons in one God means that God is one conscious Being or three, Christian theologians may be allowed to admit the paradox and make room for the mystery. Having embarked upon matters too difficult for them to understand, they can set about balancing two separate given terminologies against one another, as scientists puzzled by waves and particles may, and find illumination in both, though still unable to reconcile them in one theory.[22] As a Christian who honours the name of Einstein without claiming to comprehend his physics, I may be allowed to compare the mystery of the Trinity which confronted the first Christians with the constructive turmoil into which the theory of relativity threw the lucid world picture of Newtonian scientists.[23]

To claim the right to use this comparison, I must first acknowledge how little of the physics I can grasp. Then I may try to scramble on to whatever firm ground I can reach. If I can see glimpses of how the mystery of three Persons

[21] See above pp. 15, 17, 128.
[22] See above, pp. 32ff.
[23] Oppenheimer (1973), p. 204.

united in one God really is continuous with intelligible statements about human persons, I may hope to arrive at something like the experimental confirmation of a hypothesis.[24] To go as far as I can, not to ignore whatever data have presented themselves, and to be honest when I am stuck, should be a policy of which both scientists and theologians could approve.

The elementary notion of God the Creator as a distinct Someone matters deeply for Christians. Even if they are called naive, they cannot dispense with the idea of God as somewhat like a person with a point of view.[25] This idea of God as *Someone*, unlike the idea of God as *everywhere*, is deeply rooted in the scriptures, both the old covenant and the new; but can Christian personalism really be sustained and developed?

People who believe in a God who is enough like finite persons to be described as personal must understand that of course this proposed comparison of the Creator with human creatures is inadequate, but they need not make insuperable difficulties out of using the comparison at all. It would be defeatist to reject mystery, as if mystery had to be nonsense. If it is in order to think of people as, so to say, more personal than animals are, not less, then it can be in order to think of God as more personal than we are, not less. We are not saying that God qualifies to be somewhat like a real person, but that people qualify to be somewhat like their God.

The living God does have a point of view. God's perspective is not finite like our viewpoints but infinite, not from one place only but occupying every possible point of view in the universe. This notion is no more irreverent than other analogies from small to great. It is mind-boggling, just as some of the accepted concepts of modern physics are mind-boggling. To try to imagine that the Eye of God can both comprehend the galaxies and focus upon the minuscule details of earth is by no means a hindrance to worship.

---

[24] See above, p. 9.
[25] See above, pp. 124f.

People whose creed begins with God the Father Almighty, Maker of heaven and earth, first assert that God is transcendent, above and distinct from everything that God made. After that they can look for God as immanent, inhabiting the whole universe God made. It appears indeed that God can be particularly identified in the experience of some of the creatures who have developed into conscious persons. For Christians, the life of Jesus Christ is the paradigm case of God's real presence, on which they can build their faith in God's availability to people.

Further reading

Oppenheimer, Helen (1973) *Incarnation and immanence.* Hodder & Stoughton: e.g. Chapters 7 and 13.

Webb, C.C.J. (1918–1919) *God and personality,* Gifford Lectures vol. 1. and *Divine personality and human life ,* Gifford Lectures vol. 2. George Allen. For references see *Incarnation and immanence,* pp. 22, 34, 113–116, 201–202.

Chapter 13

God Within

... that they should seek God, in the hope that they might feel after him and find him. Yet he is not far from each one of us, for 'In him we live and move and have our being...'

Acts 17. 27–28

People who are puzzled by what God's presence could mean might follow the instruction given to examination candidates, 'compare and contrast'. If they imagine that meeting God is just like meeting another human being, they ought to look steadily and reverently at the evident contrast. But if on the other hand they are doubtful about whether meeting God makes sense at all, they can find realistic encouragement by still trying to compare. Rather than insisting only on difference, they can look at aspects of people's knowledge of one another which illuminate what knowledge of God may be like.

However mysterious spiritual presence is, it seems to have recognizable roots in human experience. Human life itself is too mysterious to be completely reduced to physics and chemistry.[1] The notion of personal encounter transcends the observable proximity of material bodies side by side, pushing each other about and sometimes colliding. The sciences have plenty of information to offer about how people interact with other people. Believers and unbelievers alike can take an interest in descriptions of light-waves and sound-waves impinging upon retinas and eardrums, hearts pumping oxygenated blood through arteries and the

---

[1]   See above, p. 120.

activity of different parts of the brain; but all along there is more to be said.

If I go shopping, or laugh at your jokes, or cast my vote, or listen to somebody playing the classical guitar, or burst into tears, or give you a birthday present, there is more going on, in an entirely natural way, than can be fully expressed in scientific formulae. The sciences cannot tell the whole story even about ordinary human communication. There are aspects of human encounters which already cannot be limited to the data which scientists handle. People are not unconnected particles nor even molecules. There is no need to go back to atomism as the default position.[2]

Although human beings are indeed distinct individuals, their independence is not the whole truth about them. Human society is more adequately characterized by using biological rather than inorganic imagery. The communications of human beings with one another are better compared with the movements of a living body than with the mechanical functioning of a working apparatus. Personal attachment means more than tying things together with knots or fixing them with glue. To do justice to human encounters and human relationships one must go beyond the neutral language of physical science by bringing in the ethical concept of *mattering*.

People are not objects placed side by side. People mind about themselves and one another and do themselves and one another good and harm. What hurts or helps one individual is not self-contained damage or benefit to that individual, but spreads out to affect the wellbeing of other people.

Adding the language of value to the language of fact[3] for talking about human interactions need not mean leaving commonsense behind and plunging into intolerable metaphysics. Both Christians and unbelievers can welcome this requirement for a moral dimension to be included in their understanding of characteristic human connectedness. People who then proceed to talk about God may humbly and happily start with their ordinary attachments to one

[2]   See above, pp. 70, 91, 119.
[3]   See above, Chapter 5.

another, and then go on to make comparisons with what they assert about their relatedness to God. They can lay a sound foundation, by allowing their hopes of encountering God to be based on their morally significant experience of encountering one another.

Sooner or later comparisons falter and contrast demands attention. Finding God is not simply like happily finding a friend in a crowded room. The idea of God as Someone whom people can meet is part of what believers find they must affirm, but only part. On the one hand Christians do envisage human knowledge of God as a kind of face-to-face relationship of people and their Maker, comparable with people's face-to-face relationship with one another. Then on the other hand they affirm the more mysterious possibility of God's Holy Spirit dwelling within them. They cannot entirely abstain from the kind of thinking which ventures upon metaphysics. Their faith encourages them from the start to go on beyond physical, ethical and even spiritual reports of personal interactions, towards a stranger theological notion of *indwelling*.

Does it make sense to say that God is within us as well as meeting us from outside? The first Christians ascribed supreme importance to their experience of finding the risen Lord, not just above them, in front of them, nor even close beside them, but somehow abiding in their hearts.[4] This concept of indwelling will not go away.[5]

Indwelling is not exactly the same as God's presence everywhere in creation. That is God's 'immanence.' The image of God's all-seeing inescapable Eye[6] is still an image of Someone who is external to human beings, looking at them. Christian thinkers must reckon with the more puzzling idea of a kind of otherness which is mysteriously compatible with oneness. The conviction of the early disciples, that separate persons can be coherently described as *abiding in* Christ and that their union with Christ unites them with

---

[4]   e.g. *Ephesians* 3.17.
[5]   See above, p. 135.
[6]   See above, p. 138.

one another is peculiarly characteristic of Christian belief. If it is given an inch, it takes an ell.

When I first discussed in print, more than thirty-five years ago,[7] what indwelling might mean, my arguments cleared my own mind but probably not other people's. The 'presenting problem' was the meaning of these odd assertions about personal unity which Christians seem to make so easily. Does the New Testament conviction that distinct people can somehow become one deepen or destroy the ordinary notion of what it means to be someone? Is the notion of union in plurality an inspiring help or a puzzling intellectual hindrance in understanding the world and living our lives?

The confidence of being *in Christ* cannot be deleted from St Paul's letters to the churches. Christians do not seem to look on his affirmation, 'it is no longer I who live, but Christ who lives in me,'[8] as a particularly hard saying. He knew what he meant from his experience and he expected his correspondents to understand him from theirs. The Gospel according to John as confidently uses the terminology of *union*. Though Christians cannot and need not assume that Chapters 14 to 17 of the fourth Gospel provide a plain historical record of the very words Jesus spoke at his last supper,[9] they can hardly reject as not even comprehensible the prayer of the Son to his Father which has meant so much to so many of his followers, 'that they may be one, even as we are one'.[10] More than three centuries later, St Augustine urged his flock, as if the idea would be plainly within their reach: 'Be you His dwelling place and He will be your dwelling place: let Him abide in you and you will abide in Him.'[11] If the notion of indwelling were lost, large areas of Christian faith would have gone.

[7] Oppenheimer (1973).
[8] *Galatians* 2.20.
[9] Bauckham (2006) offers a powerful corrective to the idea that the fourth Gospel is remote from the story it recounts.
[10] *John* 17.11, 22.
[11] St Augustine *Discourses on the Psalms* 'Fourth discourse on Psalm 30' (*Psalm* 31.22 in the usual English numbering).

Christians keep saying things like 'we, though many, are one body in Christ, and individually members one of another.'[12] They do not mean this as a casual metaphor, like saying 'We are all in one boat' or 'He is the chairman's right hand man.' Becoming a member of the Church is not just like joining a religious club.[13] There are plain statements about belonging to the church which are easy to make and comprehend, telling how much fellow members have in common and what obligations they owe to one another, but Christians must go further. They have to push the image of the Body of Christ even uncomfortably far. People's hands and feet are literally part of themselves, attached to them more fundamentally than the objects they own or even the tools they are wielding. That is the organic kind of belonging to a body which the idea of being 'one body in Christ' is meant to indicate.

Hans Andersen told the story of the Emperor's new clothes, in which nobody but a small child was frank enough to admit that he just could not see these splendid garments which everybody else was admiring.[14] His candour punctured the balloon and everyone realised that the Emperor had nothing on at all. In the twentieth century, logical positivists looked at the Christian faith and took on the role of the small child. They wanted to know whether Christian theology amounts to anything. If believers take it for granted that they are 'in Christ', but nothing they experience or fail to experience is allowed to count against this or support it, are they saying anything at all about what the world is like? If nobody could show what difference notions like 'abiding' and 'indwelling' make to the world of facts, the charge would have to stand that the enthusiastic words of theologians belong to the kind of metaphysical language which has no meaning.[15]

It is as necessary as ever for Christians to keep holding on to both plurality and unity. Commonsense is inclined to

---

[12]   *Romans* 12.4.
[13]   See above, p. 96.
[14]   Oppenheimer (1973), chapter 1.
[15]   See above, pp. 37-38; Flew (1955).

take the distinctness of persons as basic and to consider
detachment as a plainer notion than oneness, but Christians
have to take on more complication. They are convinced that
separate individuals are meant to be, not just alongside one
another, not just in touch nor even just in accord with one
another, but united together. If all this is called nonsense, it
is nonsense with so much meaning that people have lived
and died for it. There is work to be done. Efforts to speak
about what is beyond commonsense are not to be ruled out
as pointless from the start, in theology any more than in
physical science.[16]

Some believers, who have rejected the atomism which
cuts people off from one another, find it quite straightforward to move straight on, affirming not only their moral
harmony with other people but their metaphysical unity
with God. For them it does not seem a long step from the
fellow-feeling of human beings to the experience of God's
presence. *But*: to many people, including loyal Christians,
the teaching that God dwells within us, and that human
beings can 'abide' in Christ and even in one another, may
not look lucid yet, let alone illuminating and life-enhancing,
but still perplexing Their reaction is honourable and should
be taken seriously. They are not being perversely awkward
nor unfaithful. They have no wish to discourage anybody
else's simple faith.

Puzzled believers may feel inclined to hold their peace
when their fellow Christians evidently take the idea of
God's indwelling as given. They accept that their Emperor
has been wearing these theological clothes for a long time
and has felt very comfortable in them. They are his obedient
subjects, they have better manners than a small child, and
they may find it simplest and kindest to keep quiet when the
procession passes by. Rather than upset anybody, they let
themselves go along with the pious crowd, like foreign
tourists on a local feast-day, not really understanding all the
excitement nor admiring what everybody else seems to
admire, but anyway not stirring up any trouble.

---

[16] See above, p. 32.

But people who still cannot make out what the Emperor is wearing ought not always to pretend for the sake of peace that obscure notions are plain. Some cheerful Christian sermons fall flat because they are simply spinning words on biblical themes, not making an effort to describe anybody's present experience. When texts such as 'Abide in me, and I in you'[17] or 'You are all one in Christ Jesus'[18] fail to be inspiring, they can be quite depressing. Christians who have doubts find their problems exacerbated. They need pastoral care at least as much as Christians whose faith is easy. Preachers who mind about honesty would do better not to proclaim parrot-wise the ideas they have failed to fathom. They would do better still to explore them with other people.

When enquiring Christians find the theology of indwelling difficult, it would anyway be charitable rather than insincere to give it every chance to make sense. Suppose one is not learned enough to comprehend the metaphysics, nor holy enough to be vividly aware of God as present in one's own experience, it would be defeatist to opt out forthwith and leave the others to affirm their faith without expecting to share it with them. The idea of being 'in Christ' has sustained many fellow believers through the centuries. If it looks as if they are 'on to something', one can still hope to join in. The most promising start is to acknowledge one's dependence upon these companions who seem to have arrived at some distinct understanding.[19] The way people uphold one another's belief need not be a shifty kind of collusion. It may be constructive, like the temporary shuttering on a building site which supports wet concrete to keep it in shape until it has set firm.

Theologically-minded Anglicans should be glad to remember Austin Farrer, who gave a classic and vivid account of how he became able to recognize God's presence.[20] Somewhat like C.C.J. Webb,[21] he had difficulties

[17] *John* 15.4.
[18] *Galatians* 3.28.
[19] See above, p. 137.
[20] Farrer (1948), pp. 7–8, quoted in Oppenheimer (1973), pp. 51–52.
[21] Webb (1911); see above, pp. 133–34.

with the notion of *a man* and *a God* encountering one another as two separate persons, because he found that this account did not answer to his experience. He told how his efforts to pray met only with frustration, as long as he thought of God simply as another individual and imagined himself as 'set over against deity as one man faces another across a table'.

What liberated Farrer from this predicament was reading Spinoza's *Ethics.* He would not go all the way into Spinoza's pantheism, but he was enabled to stop picturing God as a separate Someone just like himself, and instead to become conscious of a sustaining Power who was 'the underlying cause' of his thinking. The kind of awareness of God for which he 'would dare to hope' was that sometimes, when he tried to pray, his thoughts would become 'diaphanous' and allow him to discern God's presence, just as 'a deep pool … permits us to see the spring in the bottom of it from which its waters rise.'

For uncertain Christians, as Austin Farrer evidently was in his youth, this is an illumination. He was not adopting at second-hand what a Christian ought to say, but offering a vivid image to capture a particular experience. His way of describing the presence of God, not generally as confronting us face to face, but as inwardly enlightening us, can bridge the centuries and bring to life the ideas of great Christian saints from St Paul and St John onwards. This kind of faith may not have anything much to say to confirmed sceptics, but puzzled would-be believers can be encouraged neither to reject the notion of personal indwelling out of hand as if it were really meaningless, nor to take for granted as if it were not mysterious. To follow this clue, to stop worrying about not being able to arrange encounters with God, and to hope to find God's Spirit indeed *inspiring* their thinking from within, can show a promising way to go.

To find such real encouragement, there is no need to escape into metaphysics. Though theology has to go beyond commonsense, it is all the better if it remains firmly grounded in commonsense. First, the difference between knowledge of God and everyday meetings with other people must duly be recognized. Images such as Farrer's 'diaphanous thought', or the Society of Friends' 'inner light', help to present the inspiration of the Spirit as still making sense. The next step is to consider whether the notion of God abiding within us can now be illuminated, not by supposing that it is like any ordinary human encounter, but still by finding valid comparisons with human encounters. The theological idea of indwelling is not straightforward meeting, but may still be rooted in the comprehensible ethical concept of people being *at one*.

The loftiest flight of unity in plurality, in the seventeenth chapter of the Fourth Gospel, is not offered as a paradoxical journey into mysticism. It is tied to a plain everyday image, the relationship of father and child. 'Holy Father, keep them in thy name, which thou hast given me, that they may be one, even as we are one.'[22] The people who will follow Christ are told that their unity is meant to be like the unity of the Son of God with God the Father. The theology need not appear so difficult when it is carefully compared after all with familiar relationships between human beings, most characteristically with the special kind of love which parents are apt to experience for their children.

To be at one with each another, not blended in some mysterious metaphysical union but joined in real moral harmony, is a hope which people can recognize and do something to accomplish in their dealings with one another. The idea of being 'in Christ' may be less obscure considered as a natural development, or indeed a supernatural development, of this known kind of unity with other people.

Abiding in one another begins to look intelligible, not as fitting souls together in baffling geometry, but as something more familiar. People are united by sharing each other's concerns. They are truly, not just fancifully, *identified* with other people when they take part in their minding. Not only parents and children, but husbands and wives, friends, colleagues and companions can start from this direction to approach the concept of people being united in their distinctness and becoming *we* rather than *I* and *I*. They do not

[22] *John* 17.11, 22.

become identical and maybe not even alike; but in their diversity they experience attachments which are more real than flights of fancy.

A comparatively modern usage may bring out what this kind of unity means. The word 'empathy' comes from the Greek *empatheia,* which means literally 'in-feeling' or 'feeling into' and has come to signify a sensitive identification with somebody else's experience.[23] Among people who are in touch with psychologists or social workers, the verb 'empathize' seems to have driven out 'sympathize' which means only 'feel with'. To realize that the best way to comprehend people is to enter attentively and patiently into their concerns makes a good corrective to over-intellectual notions about how 'minds' arrive at knowledge of 'other minds' by reasoning.

This spatial terminology is already metaphorical when it is used to describe everyday concord. Entering into people's feelings is the kind of metaphor which is able to tell the truth and which may be better than literal language for conveying the facts.[24] The metaphor of empathy shows us linking our own experience with other people's, rather than living our lives as so many isolated individuals who can get to know one another only by ratiocination.[25] For personal life, interdependence is more fundamental than separation. Affectionate communication is more significant than determined independence.

The primatologist Frans de Waal looks for the roots of human moral life in the capacities of animals for understanding one another. He notices critically[26] that most modern textbooks discussing human or animal intelligence 'fail to index empathy or sympathy', focusing on individualist criteria for brainpower, such as tool use. He has accordingly set about redressing the balance, putting stronger emphasis on 'appropriately dealing with others' and giving examples

[23] See *Twentieth century words* (Oxford University Press 1999); *New dictionary of Christian ethics and pastoral theology* (Inter-Varsity Press, 1995, pp. 343f); *Oxford companion to the mind* (1987, pp. 230–231).
[24] See above, p. 127.
[25] See above, pp. 13–14.
[26] de Waal (1996).

from the social lives of the apes he studies. However far back in the 'great chain of being'[27] empathy begins, a creature who has some capacity to be related to other creatures is beginning to be an example of what personal life means.

Since empathy matters so much, it should not be far-fetched to make the theological application and suggest that abiding 'in Christ' and in one another could be boldly elucidated today as having empathy, 'in-feeling', with Christ and with one another. Putting it this way is by no means offered as a way of watering down the Christian creeds. The hope is to light up the theology of Incarnation with an analogy, not to provide a less exacting substitute. The theological meaning is to be illuminated, not shrunk, by looking at human dealings with each other. To affirm that 'Christ was divine' means 'Christ had complete empathy with God' is like affirming that 'God was in Christ' means, 'Christ was wholly inspired by God'. Christians can make all these affirmations, provided they recognize that of course they have not said enough.

To single out empathy as the capacity of persons to identify with each other's feelings, rather than putting so much emphasis on face-to-face encounters, is a promising foundation for beginning to understand what Christians mean by 'indwelling'. Nobody need be discouraged from going on beyond this elementary starting-point into metaphysics or mysticism, but anybody who finds Christian theology puzzling could make a beginning here.

Further reading

Bauckham, Richard (2006) *Jesus and the eyewitnesses*. Eerdmans.
Flew, Anthony (1955) 'Theology and falsification' in *New essays in philosophical theology*, ed. Flew and MacIntyre. SCM Press.
Oppenheimer, Helen (1973) *Incarnation and immanence*. Hodder & Stoughton: Chapters 1 and 11.

---

[27] See Lovejoy (1953).

Chapter 14

Unity-in-Plurality

Oh I must feel your brain prompt mine
Your heart anticipate my heart …

Robert Browning, 'By the fireside'

Responsive living persons are capable of empathy. Some-body might object, Why complicate what is not obscure by re-wording it in sociological jargon? The Lord did not tell people to empathize with one another but to love their neighbours as themselves. Surely basic New Testament *agape*, translated into plain English as *love*, should be good enough for twenty-first century Christians? St Paul writing to the Corinthians[1] affirmed that love never ends. The Fourth Gospel elaborated this teaching in terms of love which abides.[2]

If all this really is plain and not obscure, and followers of Christ can simply set about living by it, so well and good. They can put aside difficult ideas about 'indwelling' and try by God's grace to put Christian love into practice. 'See how these Christians love each other' was at first not said in irony. But sometimes Christians give the impression that what they mean by loving one another is itself a difficult idea, revealed to babes maybe but hidden from the wise and prudent.[3]

It would appear that loving other people just as one loves oneself must be counted as part of the whole package which the 'Creed of St Athanasius' alarmingly describes as 'the

---

[1]   *1 Corinthians* 13.
[2]   Especially in *John* 15; see above, pp. 142ff.
[3]   *Matthew* 11.25.

Catholick Faith: which except a man believe faithfully, he cannot be saved.' Yet on consideration, is love any easier than indwelling? Does unselfish altruism even make sense? Are human beings generous only to boost their own self-esteem? Is being kind essentially a transaction for earning kindness in return? Are people always merely trying to hide their egotism, even from themselves? Some people seem naturally capable of unselfconscious goodwill. Others try to work it out and find that the more they theorize about the competing claims of the self and the others, the more difficult it all gets and the more selfishness seems to win.

Many disciples from St Paul and St John onwards have been helped to grasp the meaning of love by thinking of people abiding in Christ and Christ abiding in people. Christians are to aspire to a kind of unity which breaks through the commonsense boundaries which keep people apart. This idea of *indwelling* is a central theme for Christians, not a decorative garnish. Rather than putting the notion aside as obscure, they have taken it to elucidate what Christian love means. But unless this vocabulary does turn out to illuminate the ordinary ways human beings talk about loving one another, it will be a hindrance not a help. When the language of unity which is supposed to mean so much is bandied carelessly about, it loses its vigour and becomes exhausted, saying everything or nothing and collapsing into insignificance. No wonder puzzled believers are tempted to ignore the perplexity they feel and take it for granted that everyone else understands what the early Christians who used this theological language so happily were trying to say. Of course we can all see how magnificent the Emperor's new clothes are: until the small child speaks up.[4]

The concept of 'empathy', *in-feeling,* can come to the rescue. By indicating a familiar human capacity, this metaphor offers to shed light on what the grand Christian claims about 'indwelling' might mean. To speak about people as entering into one another's experience suggests a way of

[4]   See above, pp. 144f.

understanding the unity of separate persons, by picking out a recognizable feature of personal life more definite than general goodwill.

The notion is usable because there are plenty of ordinary examples of it. Empathy is more than standing side by side as physical things do, more than being merely aware of one another's presence, more than being able to predict what another person will do next. It is seeing the world from other people's points of view, catching their fear or boredom, their amusement or their happiness, wincing at their pain and sighing with their relief. Empathy can be wholly unsophisticated. Children sometimes go straight to the core of an adult trouble. There are many anecdotes about horses who seem to pick up their riders' feelings; and dogs who appear to grasp that something stressful is going on in a human household.

The capacity for understanding, for experiencing other people's joys and sorrows, indeed for sharing their lives and saying 'we', is indeed as an ordinary part of what it means to be *someone*. Empathy ought not to be treated as an optional extra which only specially sensitive people can achieve. Though some people have the gift of empathy more than others, and many of us could try harder to develop it, a human being who lacks empathy has a definite disability.

People's practical moral awareness does amount to something more than existing alongside one another. We do have a positive notion of people being at one in their diversity; and 'empathy' is one way of expressing this. As a basis for understanding, to say 'both this — and that' is generally more promising than to insist on 'either–or'. The perception that individual lives can be distinct *and* connected, not sometimes one and sometimes the other but both at once, enlarges the idea of being someone. There is more to anyone's experience than one conscious animated body interacting mechanically with other conscious animated bodies like the moving parts of an apparatus.[5]

---

[5] See above, p. 141.

It is sometimes worth repeating the obvious to avoid mis-leading detours. People find themselves linked together morally. Of course it is a platitude to assert that human relationships have an ethical dimension, but it is a significant platitude, not a knee-jerk cliché. The everyday recognition that I am not isolated, that here and now there is somebody else making a real difference to my world, turns out to be deeper and stranger than a plain account of the physical data can express.

The scientific narrative about what physical events are going on still underlies accounts of fellow-feeling and is as reliable as ever. Believers along with unbelievers can establish the material facts about persons and explore what they are, physically, chemically, biologically and psychologically. This is a thoroughly valid and useful enterprise: so long as people remain aware that there is more to be understood. The subject-matter investigated by these useful and interesting studies is not merely an assortment of inanimate objects but individual living people, who matter more to themselves and one another than data to be inspected.

Theologians should not proceed to claim 'empathy' as if it were their own registered brand name for labelling what Christians mean by loving other people. The current ordinary use of this concept provides one convenient approach to human moral understanding. The language of empathy brings out how the love which people talk about so easily is not an abstract idea but has a purchase on reality.

This route into ethical thinking is indeed convenient, because empathy is a practical notion, not grounded in high metaphysical speculations but in recognizable facts of experience. It does make sense for distinct persons to be 'at one' without their own identities being mingled and lost. People who have realised that it will not do to think of themselves as unattached self-sufficient atoms[6] can attend hopefully to *unity in plurality* as a promising slogan. They can be ready to recognize ordinary examples of a kind of union 'which does

---

[6] See above, pp. 70, 91, 118.

not destroy but fulfils the distinctive character' of separate people who belong together.[7]

Christians can proceed to apply this way of thinking about persons as united by love to the mysterious doctrine that God's own being is threefold.[8] The dogma of the Holy Trinity appears less baffling when ethics are allowed to shed light on the theology. The moral conviction that human persons are not detached atoms can illuminate the theological conviction that the One God in whose image they are created is not a detached Person. The invitation to believe in God as a Unity of Father, Son and Spirit looks less like a threateningly incomprehensible mathematical challenge when it is interpreted by the conviction that 'God is love'; and 'God is love' is interpreted by the conviction that part of what love means is shared experience.

The foundation of Christian personalism is the claim that people are created in the image and likeness of God.[9] The moral assertion that relatedness is the point of personal life rests upon the doctrine that the Creator is Three Persons in One God, not separate but united. The human persons we know are godlike in their capacity to be connected by love.

One of many everyday images which can illuminate the doctrine of the Trinity is the union of marriage, in which two people truly become one entity without losing their separate identities.[10] Legally, morally and theologically they belong together. 'We' is decidedly as real as 'I'.[11] A husband and a wife are united by a strong permanent bond; but still nobody thinks that they have become one human being. Christians can use human matrimony as a particularly apt analogy for helping them to understand the theology of divine Persons belonging to one another and acting together.

Believers may constructively go on to point out that spouses are not exclusively occupied with adoring each

[7]   Well expressed long ago by A.M. Allchin, in a review in *Theology* (October 1965, p. 489); Oppenheimer (1973), p. 204 n. 4.
[8]   See above, pp. 130ff.
[9]   *Genesis* 1.26.
[10] See Oppenheimer (1971), p. 127.
[11] See above, pp. 16, 66.

other. Their love does not characteristically remain self-enclosed and inward-looking. On the contrary, the role of the pairbond in the evolution of the human species is that a man and a woman shall be fruitful and multiply. On the one hand, children are additional to the lives of their parents, who have first chosen each other for their very own. On the other hand, new human beings characteristically become the pairbond's fulfilment. In some such way as this, beloved creatures find themselves both extra and made welcome to the plural and united life of God.[12]

It is fair to acknowledge that the argument up to now has emphasized the threeness more than the oneness of the God who loves. It has tended towards what has been called the 'social theory' of the Trinity.[13] To a Christian personalist, the belief that there are personal relationships within God's own nature[14] is decidedly more attractive than an austere belief in one sole self-sufficient God. Of course it is salutary to remember that 'God is not a committee'.[15] Seizing hold of one side of the truth is just the way that heresy is typically formed. But still Christian theologians must describe their hope and try to explain it in the words which make most sense to them. Their calling is to bear witness, with all diffidence, to what they believe to be true, one-sidedly if necessary, realizing all the time how partial their statements are, and not ignoring the demand to give reasons for having any faith at all.[16]

Nobody will grasp what Christians are talking about, unless they can offer some indication of how the theological arithmetic of unity-in-plurality can be applied in reality. Theologians who are trying to spell out the meaning of what they believe can begin to justify their chosen explanation by calling attention to why this matters and why anyone should mind about it. Ethical thinking can bring the paradoxical mathematics down to earth .

---

[12] See above, p. 136.
[13] See Oppenheimer (1973), p. 204.
[14] See above, pp. 131, 135.
[15] Baker (1970), p. 312.
[16] *1 Peter* 3.15.

Problems about obscure or technical notions become both more significant and more possible to solve, when they take shape as moral enquiries concerning the choices people have to make and the attitudes they must take up in their ordinary lives. People ask questions because they need answers. Theological questions like 'How can distinct persons "abide in" one another?' make sense in something like the way questions of moral philosophy make sense, when they are found to have practical application. Do we find *values* existing in the real world or must we make them up for ourselves? What has *virtue* to do with making people happy? What counts as *happiness* and who counts as a *person*? Then likewise: What difference does it make if someone is 'in Christ'? It is when theorizing becomes ethical exploration that it justifies itself as concrete and relevant.

It is time to pick up and emphasize a recurring pattern in the arguments so far. Metaphysical debates are supposed to be irrelevant and unreal, and practical people treat them as unimportant; but when the abstract questions turn into enquiries about what makes people's lives worthwhile, then they come to life.[17] A notorious philosophical problem which has turned out to yield to this way of approaching it is the question about 'our knowledge of other minds'.[18] Solipsism could not be refuted theoretically, by supposing oneself to set off alone in the world needing arguments to prove that other people exist. Instead it makes good sense to begin by taking our stand on familiar human relationships; and so to recognize that our known capacity to communicate with one another is the best clue to the nature and needs of the people we are. Keeping in touch is part of what it means to be a person, not a specialized achievement.

Similarly, metaphysical problems about the nature and status of 'the soul'[19] can be found less puzzling and baffling when they come alive as problems of ethics. People may feel sure that they are more than their bodies, but they do need an answer for philosophers who ask, What is this 'more'? If

[17] See above, p. 7.
[18] See above, Chapter 2.
[19] See above, pp. 6, 8, 25f, 80.

the answer has to be that a 'soul' is a sort of thing, independent of the body, which somehow we can never quite catch, the down-to-earth materialists will hardly be convinced that the search for souls is an enterprise worth pursuing. Why worry about how many angels could dance on a pin when we could be trying to find out how to cure cancer?

The questions about the presence or absence of a soul do not look like real questions unless they are seen to take their rise in everyday reality. Then they need answers.[20] When does am embryo become *someone?* When did I begin?[21] Has that man or that woman ceased to exist? Are abortion[22] and euthanasia[23] always wrong? Is *in vitro* fertilization an ethical way of honouring human life? When there are moral decisions to be made, there is some point in asking about realities which are not merely physical.

If someone's 'soul' is not imagined as a separate detachable entity, but considered practically as the physical and spiritual person taken as a whole, then the intellectual conundrum, 'Do people have souls and are souls sacred?' becomes a practical moral question, which can be expressed as, 'Is there anyone here and what ought we to do about it?' If this group of living cells or that unconscious person is *someone*, or perhaps is not someone yet or not someone any more, what follows about how all the people concerned ought to be treated?

Then, when theological perplexity arises about how persons can be united in their diversity, Christians who handle the questions according to this pattern should find that the paradoxes begin to appear less baffling. Problems about how to think of people as both one and many develop into problems about what people are doing and what they ought to do. If what Christians try to say about indwelling turns out to make a difference to practical morality, their assertions look much less like nonsense. Live ethics has more substance than speculative metaphysics.

---

[20] See above, pp. 7–8.
[21] See Ford (1988).
[22] See above, Chapter 8.
[23] See above, Chapter 6.

'Abide in me, and I in you', in its context in the Fourth Gospel, is about how Christians are to be like the growing branches of a vine, bearing good fruit.[24] If people take heed of this image, it will affect their lives. Affirmations about two people being *at one* with each other, or about the union of the Father with the Son, however hard these are to express in plain prose, are candidates for being positively significant statements because their truth or falsehood is found to matter morally. Announcements which may look like unintelligible riddles or unsupported assertions, even if they are taken straight from the Bible, come to life when they shed light on what matters in people's daily lives. It is all the better if they not only shed cool light, but also kindle the warmth of minding about one another.

This is the context in which the promisingly ordinary psychological notion of empathy comes to the rescue of the strange theological notion of indwelling. The idea of sensitivity to someone else's experience, taking part in someone else's minding, opens up the meaning of the traditional assertions about abiding in love or about being 'in Christ'. Here is a recognizable way of understanding what unity in plurality can mean, which matters enough to mean something.

This language which the first Christians used so readily is founded on the recognizable and even familiar possibility of a kind of worthwhile harmony between persons which is still compatible with their real distinctness. 'I' is not lost but is positively enhanced when people enter rewarding relationships. When they say 'we' they can truly speak for the others, but they are still separate enough to say 'you' to each other. People who think about ethics can explore the meaning of this kind of unity without being plunged into metaphysical obscurity.

People's presence to one another amounts to more than their plain physical presence as objects side by side; and the time-honoured theological idea of 'indwelling' provides a terminology for taking notice of this 'more'. This way of

[24] *John* 15.4.

speaking is metaphorical, but it is serious metaphor[25] which is playing a usefully distinct role. The Emperor can try on his new clothes and see whether they are thick enough to keep him warm.

Further reading

Oppenheimer, Helen (1971) 'Marriage as illustrating some Christian doctrines' Appendix 4 to *Marriage, Divorce and the church*, The report of the Commission on the Christian doctrine of marriage. SPCK.

---

[25]   See above, p. 127.

III. GENEROSITY

Chapter 15

Built-in Value

> ... but for our ceaseless labour ... the Church of England might have become a perfect hotbed of charity and humility.
>
> <div align="right"><i>The Screwtape letters</i>, Chapter 16</div>

Materialism has been left a long way back.[1] It is impossible and unnecessary to reduce all truth to physics and chemistry. In the everyday world we inhabit together, most people seem to discover more reality than physical science encompasses. Confidence that they are wrong is a stance which is no more obvious than confidence that they are right. Whatever transcendence may mean, some people who are neither naive nor eccentric keep finding that the effort to talk about it coherently is rewarding.

Ordinary prosaic experience often has enough moral significance included in it to make scientific analysis inadequate. Plain facts are not all value-free.[2] People recognize goodness and badness which are built in to human life all along, without needing to be added on to the real world by somebody choosing to think like that. Friendship is a blessing; a piece of work is well done, an accident is a disaster; cheating is culpable, casual teasing is unkind; doing one's best to help is praiseworthy. To refrain from counting ethical assertions like these as statements of real facts is not a mark of intelligence and could be a mark of insensitivity. Value judgements can be received as straightforwardly true, not demoted to be matters of opinion. Reasonable peo-

---

[1] See above, pp. 32–33.
[2] See above, pp. 34f; and further reading, below.

ple expect to be confronted by authentic moral claims which are part of their data and are not for them to invent or select.

The dread gulf which is supposed to separate the familiar land of *is* from the uncharted land of *ought* is really spanned by sturdy bridges.[3] The places where the fact/value gap is easiest to cross are located where there are people, who turn out to belong on both sides. People can be seen as objects bumping into other objects, but they are also conscious subjects who take heed of one another. A person is a gateway where mattering has access into the world. To acknowledge somebody's presence is to set foot on a bridge linking facts with values, where what *ought to be* can be reached from what *is*.

A person is, so to say, a foothold for value. The people we encounter every day matter, and we know this for a fact. Moral thinking can get started without having to plunge down into metaphysical depths. We can look on ordinary human beings as meeting-places for 'is' and 'ought', commonsense and mystery, science and theology. We may like to express this conviction by saying that the notion of *spirit* comes into its own here.[4] There is no obligation to adopt that particular terminology, but using it is a way of keeping one's mind open to the possibility that there really is *more* in life than prosaic commonsense might expect.

It is worth reiterating that thinking of people as more than physical objects does not mean chasing after elusive ghosts along the ancient path marked dualism.[5] The understanding that some*one* is more than merely some*thing* is not best achieved by taking an individual to pieces to hunt for the hidden treasure called 'the soul'. Expecting to find spirits apart from bodies is not a promising way to catch sight of valuable people. The person who matters is indeed one whole, really bodily and really spiritual, living in one shared world with other whole persons.[6]

---

[3] See above, pp. 45–46.
[4] See above, pp. 8, 23, 28 (top), 33, 36, 42 (foot), 47f.
[5] See above, pp. 18, 22, 28, 56, 118.
[6] See above, Chapter 3.

Discerning the spiritual nature of people does not mean going back to the idea that everyone owns a sort of thing called an immortal soul. There is no need to imagine that somewhere, in some hiding place, each of us has a precious metaphysical item which gives us our value now and is guaranteed to survive when the body dies. The 'immortality of the soul' is not the most satisfactory way of expressing the worth of human life now; nor is it what Christians need to give them hope for the future. Practical belief in the 'life of the world to come' is belief in the renewing of complete people who in some way will still be physical.[7] They will indeed be spirits but they will not be spooks.

The traditional language of souls provides one way of attending to spiritual reality beyond physics. It is not the only way of speaking which sets aside dogmatic materialism and makes room for values. The increasingly familiar terminology of empathy[8] is especially convenient, for making the link between neutral scientific statements and statements about what people find worthwhile. Empathy is a concept which is well understood and taken for granted in the context of social workers and their clients, but which is usefully applied more widely than its professional setting. This language draws attention to people's characteristic capacity for minding about themselves and one another. Responsiveness[9] is a desirable and practical endowment about which physics and chemistry cannot tell the whole story.

A warning against impertinence is needed. If well-meaning people, confident in the virtue of their empathy, try to walk uninvited into other people's lives, they run the risk of infringing their privacy and undermining their dignity. The Christian terminology of entering and abiding might seem to purport burgling and squatting rather than fellowship. Talk about empathy is not the answer to every question about how people ought to relate to one another, any more than talk about the sacredness of people's souls solves all

---

[7]   See above, p. 29.
[8]   See above, p. 149.
[9]   See Oppenheimer (2006), pp. 49–50.

problems about how people ought to be treated. The language of empathy is most promising as a more precise and encouraging corrective to piously high-flown language about unity and rash assumptions about love.

People of goodwill in the twenty-first century speak naturally about sharing somebody else's experience. They may be near to the meaning of the New Testament theologians who spoke naturally about *koinonia*, communion.[10] Ancient and contemporary moral thinkers alike can start with a plain vocabulary of participating, partnership, having in common, and both may be able to let these ordinary ways of thinking develop into deeper but no less practical ideas about fellowship, becoming one and abiding in love.

People who want to contribute to moral discussion can enrich their vocabulary by playing with language, trying out the available words for characterizing human moral life. They can hope to discover experimentally whether favourite ways of talking about how people overcome their separation and achieve unity do or do not make good sense. By being prepared to use and reflect together on the ancient and modern keywords which cluster around the idea of responsiveness, thinking Christians could themselves be providing practical examples of what empathy means. The words they use could turn out to foster a frame of mind ready to be responsive to what other people are trying to convey.

Theologians may proceed from here to explore distinctive Christian teaching about how to be someone among others. They can look in detail at the ways believers have learned to think about the nature, value and relationships of persons. They can apply these thoughts to their God as well as to God's creatures, taking up and trying to explain technical terms like Trinity, Incarnation and Atonement. They may embark upon adventurous metaphysical journeys and they will certainly need large supplies of philosophical, historical and linguistic expertise, not to mention

---

[10] See above, p. 97.

faith, hope and charity, if their efforts are to succeed in encouraging themselves and their fellow believers.

Once again, ethical enquiries may be more manageable, less specialized and more practical than the technicalities.[11] The recurrent notion of *something more* is particularly needed by people who are concerned with what persons are and what they ought to be. At least a person is more than a biological organism. Christian thinkers may be able to manage without the particular language of the soul, but they will not be able to manage for long without a language which lets in value. But further: a person, who is more than merely physical, turns out to be somebody who is more than merely moral. What matters to human beings goes beyond their rights and the duties they owe. People's experience becomes life-enhancing when it expands creatively beyond the basic obligation to keep the laws of right and wrong.

Human beings find it surprisingly tempting to restrict their moral lives. It looks like commonsense to tidy up ethics by sorting out the claims we have to recognize into two plain categories, demands which are compulsory and demands which are optional. The exercise of reducing morality to 'Yes, you must' and 'No, you must not', with 'Yes, you may' as a safety-valve, is a trap constantly lying in wait for people who want to be good. Once they start seriously considering what goodness really is, they need to move forward by way of a critique of legalism.

The way to escape from legalism is not just to abandon the repressive rules. People who try that route run the contrary risk of disregarding order, losing touch with justice and ignoring what is properly due to people. When intolerant assumptions have rigidly held sway for too long, they suddenly give way to relaxed permissiveness, which turns out to be no more conducive to solid human happiness. The 1960s were a time like that, when 'to be young was very

---

[11] See above, p. 7.

heaven'[12] and old tyrannies were swept away, but revolutionary enthusiasm did not really bring in a golden age.

It is nearer to the spirit of the Gospel not to set about knocking away the foundations, to build on a solid underlying tradition of right and wrong and to learn to enlarge it into an ethic of generosity. That is, as usual, to look for both/and, not either/or. The Lord came, not to destroy the law, but to fulfil it,[13] and what he required was not less but more. Responsiveness is a key to unlock this 'more'. To discover the moral possibility of willingly transcending what the law demands can be a natural not an extraordinary feat for human beings.

People's happiness depends upon learning this, but it is a sad indictment of believers how difficult a lesson they sometimes find this teaching. They can hardly take in that when a sinner encounters the Lord he is not told to kneel down in the dust, but is sent straight away to prepare a welcoming feast.[14] They feel a little uncomfortable that when the Lord is a guest at a wedding he does not preach a sermon about the duties of matrimony, but concerns himself, as Austin Farrer pointed out, with providing an extravagant supply of wine.[15]

Certainly the lesson of generosity can be hard. Faithful Christians are not being unreasonable if they persist in feeling 'It's not fair' if the fresh new workers are given the same wages as the ones who have borne the heat of the day.[16] Disciples of Christ want to uphold moral standards and it worries them when the Father of the prodigal son hardly waits for his child to say he is sorry before celebrating his return.[17] Indeed these outcomes are not fair, but neither the virtuous elder brother nor the irresponsible younger brother can enter the kingdom of heaven without having come to see the limits of fairness.

---

[12] Wordsworth, on the early days of the French Revolution, *The Prelude*, Book XI, ll. 108–109.
[13] *Matthew* 5.17.
[14] *Luke* 19.2.
[15] *John* 2. 1–11; see Farrer (1970).
[16] *Matthew* 20.1–16.
[17] *Luke* 15.11–32.

Even setting limits to fairness is not the whole point, if that means only drawing the limits further on than the ones where we began. The dutiful calculation 'When I have counted up to seventy times seven, then I can be angry with my brother'[18] is even more unsafe than casual misdoings. There is no generosity in the stance which says, 'Now that will do. I have done more than they could expect. I'm not claiming to be a saint. Extremes like that are not really my line.'

There are two different frames of mind in which a culprit may try to stave off blame. 'You can't say I overstepped the limits. I'm not at fault,' takes a stand on law and must abide by law. Without a correct acquittal, there is no alternative but to condemn the offender. On the other hand, 'I know what I did was unacceptable. I wish I could have found another way. Please understand that this was too much for me,' allows mercy to have a hearing. Christian moralists can still not expect easy solutions when they have to deal with repentant sinners, but they are not forced to give legalism the last word.

A just critic of legalism ought to make sure that law is given its due place and indeed can be grateful for its protection. Christians ought not to patronize the psalmists, as if they had missed the point of the Gospel when they delighted in the law of the Lord and found it sweeter than honey and the honeycomb.[19] What the psalmists were looking for was not authorized selfishness but a way of living which would glorify God. They could still fall into legalism, if they went on to think that their way of living was a guarantee of rectitude; or if they set about harshly imposing upon other people what was a delight to them.

Human beings who are social creatures living in communities need the convenience of rules and cannot do without them; but there is more; and the 'more' makes life worth living. We can do better than priggish 'works of supererogation', which still calculate legalistically what is due and then carefully go beyond that in order to lay a claim to righteousness. We can characterize the morality we need as an ethic of

[18]   *Matthew* 18.21f.
[19]   *Psalms* 1.2; 19.10.

generosity; or we could adopt and adapt the classical notion of *magnanimity*, greatness of soul; or better still we may learn from the first Christians the meaning of *charity*. All this can be put into practical shape as an ethic of *welcome*, people welcoming one another as they believe God welcomes them.[20] Such a morality is not likely to be thoroughly learnt by being taught in the form of rules to keep. The Lord was not wont to legislate, but rather told stories; and the stories build up into a picture of what the Kingdom of heaven is like.

This way of approaching Christian ethics by-passes biblical fundamentalism. There is no need to suppose that unless some particular story preserves the very words Jesus uttered on a given day, its teaching is not to be trusted. The useful concept of 'ben trovato',[21] 'well found', is what his followers need and what the Gospels provide: samples of his characteristic teaching, vivid, true to life and authoritative. Christians can take these stories to heart, be judged by them, be inspired by them and try in his name to put their lessons into practice.

The foundation of Christian ethics is the God who entered into human life, just as the foundation of the ethics of the old Covenant is the God who brought the children of Israel out of Egypt.[22] A besetting aberration of God's people throughout all their history has been legalism, but the morality they have followed at their best has been a grateful morality of response to the God who has constantly come to their rescue.

Further reading

The whole list given for Chapter 5 is relevant here, especially Oppenheimer (1975; 1983; 1995/2003).

---

[20] See above, pp. 100, 103, 136, 156, and chapter 19 below.
[21] I think I owe this notion to Professor Basil Mitchell, in discussion about ten years ago.
[22] *Exodus* 20. 2–17

Chapter 16

Children of God

The Father: of an infinite Majesty

Te Deum

The plain difference between a living person and a thing is that a person responds to events.[1] Responsiveness at its simplest means the capacity to react to pleasure or pain. On this capacity depends the possibility of minding about what happens, experiencing joy and sorrow and living a life. Somebody who was all alone could be responsive in a limited and elementary way. But responsiveness as the foundation of ethics has the central meaning of response to one another. Though people sometimes become isolated, characteristically they belong together. Recognizing one another's responses is the usual foundation of their moral lives.

The idea of responsiveness soon leads to the moral idea of *responsibility*. People are accountable to one another, both negatively and positively, responsible for not doing other people harm and often responsible for helping them. Some people have particular responsibilities for looking after other people, arising from particular roles. They are spouses, parents, grown up children, teachers, doctors and nurses, secretaries, cooks, bodyguards, pastors. In some of these capacities they become morally and even legally accountable for the lives and welfare of their charges. They are not allowed to say, 'that's not my business'.

Christians extend responsibility to one another more widely, even to a limitless extent, by asserting that we are all

[1]   See above, p. 1; Oppenheimer (2006) pp. 40f.

brothers and sisters, because God is our heavenly Father. The Creed starts here: 'I believe in one God the Father Almighty.' Belief in the heavenly Father was the foundation of the teaching of Christ, before he died and rose again and became part of the creed himself. To put this doctrine of God first is a wholesome corrective to the almost idolatrous temptation for some Christian believers to by-pass God the Father and concentrate their piety entirely upon Jesus, their good and lovable Master who once lived in Galilee and now lives in heaven. Everyone who takes to heart what the Lord Jesus did teach, in all the accounts we have of his life, can say, 'I am someone who is a child of God.'[2]

Anybody may embrace the ideal that human beings are one family, and live by it consciously or unconsciously; but Christians are to draw their human goodwill explicitly from its transcendent source. The basis of the Christian ethic of generosity[3] is 'the God and Father of our Lord Jesus Christ.'[4] Christians believe that they are given authority to call God 'Father' by 'the Spirit himself bearing witness with our spirit that we are children of God.'[5] They are bound to apply this conviction that they are God's own family to themselves and also to one another.

It is easier to put our highest values into practice by responding to being loved than by making efforts of will. The notion that the almighty and holy God acknowledges human creatures as children and heirs is a doctrine of encouragement. This doctrine of God's Fatherhood as the basis of Christian morality is far from belittling God's sacredness and might. The more hopeful this ethic is, the more it is also awesome.

Now feminists feel restive. Since Christians are determined to call God 'Father', must it follow that the Christian faith is irredeemably patriarchal? While traditional Christians are naturally reluctant to jettison their authorized

---

[2]   e.g. especially *Mark* 11.23; *Matthew* 5–7 (the 'Sermon on the Mount'); *Luke* 11.12; *John* 17.11,24; 20.17; see above, p. 148.
[3]   See above, p. 166.
[4]   *1 Peter* 1.3; *2 Corinthians* 11.31.
[5]   *Romans* 8.15–16.

image of God, feminist Christians suggest correcting the language of Fatherhood and even replacing it by the language of Motherhood.

Julian of Norwich long ago used the robust image of 'our Mother Christ'[6] less contentiously than some Christian women today. 'God almighty is our loving Father, and God all wisdom is our loving Mother, with the love and the goodness of the Holy Spirit, which is all one God, one Lord.'[7] *The Oxford dictionary of the Christian church* points out 'her uniquely unsentimental use of the fairly common medieval idea of Christ as mother'.[8] Christians today ought to be grateful for ways of speaking about God which correct the ingrained sexism which afflicts the human race and not least the Christian church. There are also reasons for caution.

At least it matters that we should not proceed to reinforce sexist stereotypes instead of avoiding them, by setting up the gentle nurturing God the Mother as a rival to the stern judgmental God the Father. God is One.[9] There is no battle going on between God's kindness and God's holiness. It may be well be salutary to take up sometimes describing God as motherly; but the good news of the new covenant is not to be summarized as, 'Come here and let me kiss it better but you mustn't do that again or your Father will be angry when he comes home.'

It is the one God who is 'the high and lofty One who inhabits eternity',[10] who has a 'mighty arm' to defend his, or her, people[11] and who wants to gather her, or his, children together 'as a hen gathers her brood under her wings'.[12] Christians may find it enlightening to try out 'Father, 'Mother' and 'Parent', by turns. Any of these can identify aspects of God's glory, but the one which definitely rooted in the teaching of Christ is Father. Loyal traditionalists have

---

[6]   *Showings*, Long text, chapter 58.
[7]   ibid.
[8]   3rd edition (1997), p. 911.
[9]   *Deuteronomy* 6.4.
[10]   *Isaiah* 57.15
[11]   e.g. *Psalm* 89.14.
[12]   *Matthew* 23.37 / *Luke* 13.34.

good reason to give priority to this image. They should still realize that all talk about God is picture-language and not dare to treat any single picture as if it were complete. A variety of images can complement one another, as in the resolution of George Herbert's poem 'The collar':

> Me thoughts I heard one calling, *Child!*
> And I replied, *My Lord!*

A practical reason for not letting the Mother image take over is that the human reality it immediately brings to mind is the particular bond between a woman and her young children. Whether we like it or not, that stage is going to be outgrown. The relationship of mother and baby is as temporary as it is fundamental. When people are hurt or afraid, or when they are rash and over-confident, the cherishing Mother who knows best is an image of God which can fit their need. But human mothers have to learn to let go. For women, the route to adult parental love goes by way of birth and weaning which are experiences of separation. By applying Christian theology to the human blessing of motherhood, they may recognize an example of the good news that people receive what is most worth having by giving it up and not grabbing it.

The image of God as the nurturing Mother, taken on its own, well emphasizes the teaching that Christians are to have secure faith like little children, but it may have the effect of postponing indefinitely St Paul's encouraging hope that Christians are growing up to maturity, 'to the measure of the stature of the fullness of Christ'.[13] The maternal image could play into the hands of hostile critics if it fails to allow for coming-of-age and gives the impression that the Gospel endorses permanent childish dependence.

The paternal image can have a wider range. In practice, it is less closely identified with one particular parental role. As an image of God, 'Father' comprehends the ancient reverence for the authority of parents upheld in the Fifth Commandment, and also, alongside that severity, the trustful everyday 'Abba' of Jewish family life. To take up trans-

---

[13] *Ephesians* 4.13–15; cf. *1 Peter* 2.2.

lating 'Abba' as 'Daddy' or 'Dad' would be a somewhat foolish gimmick; but to play with that notion at times might put more heart into diffident faith. The unceremoniousness of 'Abba' could puncture the kind of vaguely pompous piety which takes 'Our Father' for granted as the proper way for Christians to address God, while hardly considering how much it means to speak to God like this.[14] To imagine God the Almighty Creator as really like a human parent picks out a recognizable filial relationship of honour and love which does not need to be outgrown. The point is not the gender but the familiarity.

The analogy signifies more than pastoral encouragement for timid Christians to approach God simply and comfortably in their prayers. To call God Father makes a bold theological statement about God's own character. Christians affirm that the way men and women want to have families is an image of the way God wants to have a family. Human beings truly matter to God as children matter to their parents; and belonging to God's family is a good image for this. I hope that this emphasis on God's creative love is in line with Marianne Meye Thompson's careful discussion of God and gender in *The promise of the Father*.[15]

God's children should not suppose that father-love is more divine than mother-love. They ought to avoid the plain sexism which is called 'patriarchy'. It should be easier for Christians to avoid patriarchy than it was for pagans who worshipped Zeus the Father of gods and men. Christians assert first that God is Father but do not stop there, They fill out this faith by their doctrine of the Holy Trinity. They do not proclaim a Deity who is a male person, but one God revealed as three Persons. God creates, God saves and God inspires; and these three roles express the same love. There is plenty of scope for saying 'both/and' about God's plural unity and using feminine as well as masculine images for exploring its meaning.

Christians have found variegated human analogies to shed light on their doctrine of the Holy Trinity. The Gospel

[14] See above, pp. 156, 170.
[15] Thompson (2000), pp. 178–183.

image of the one loving Father can be illuminated, and certainly not contradicted, by the image of human parents united in upholding one another. The fatherly God neither excludes nor competes with a motherly God. Fathers and mothers protect and provide, nourish and comfort, and these are not separate enterprises.

Biology and history have encouraged male and female human beings to specialize; but a promising result of feminism has been to allow parents more flexibility in their dealings with their children than men and women have been permitted in the past. Fathers are allowed and encouraged to be more approachable and do some of the nurturing. We have the opportunity now to enlarge our understanding of God's love by comparing it freshly with the ways parents love their children. Some Christians feel encouraged to enrich the terminology of divine fatherhood with the terminology of divine motherhood. Others may prefer to keep to the traditional language but use it more carefully and sensitively.

However people extend the analogy, it begins with children relying on their parents' care and parents cherishing the particular value of each beloved child. Not limited to infancy, the analogy can be explored by considering how human family relationships mature. When the love of parents and children develops into reciprocal dependable faithfulness, spreading out characteristically to the further blessing of new generations, parenthood offers the most promising picture of the love of God.

Christians are able to apply parental imagery confidently to God's dealings with us, because this language is directly rooted in the teaching of Jesus that indeed this is the best way to think about God. We can spell out Christian theology by speaking of the heavenly Father, who wants these beloved children to do well, who is on their side, who is not trying to catch them out, but who may be formidably angry with them when they do badly, just because they matter so much. Julian of Norwich was not theorizing but relating the visions that had been shown to her, when she described compellingly God's delight and God's minding. 'We are his

joy, we are his reward, we are his glory, we are his crown …
And with this our good Lord said most blessedly, "Look
how much I loved you"'.[16]

It is a constant temptation for Christian preachers to wax
eloquent in platitudes about God's fatherly love, assuming
that we all know what our heavenly Father's care means, to
the comfort of some good Christians but the discourage-
ment of others. The image needs careful and exact application in the light of the whole Gospel. In particular, belief in
God the Father needs to be applied as hopefully to God who
presides as to God who protects. The images of Judge and
Parent should be juxtaposed not contrasted, as indeed they
are in the *Book of Common Prayer*, where the people confess
their sins to God who is both 'Maker of all things, Judge of
all men' and 'most merciful Father.'[17]

It is straightforward for Christians to think of God as their
Father when life is going well and they can give thanks for
God's grace. It is just as natural to cry out to our Father for
help like frightened children when things are going badly.
When people are doing their best, they readily suppose that
their Father will be pleased with them. But the perception
which Christians who want to be good are more likely to
miss is that God is just as much their own Father when they
have done poorly.

When believers are conscious of sin and need to be forgiven, the God they too easily imagine confronting them at
last is not an affectionate parent but a terrifying Lord. They
trust that He will have mercy and they hope that He will let
them off from punishment. They think remorsefully, 'How
dreadful to have broken God's holy law', or 'How mortify-
ing to be so disgraced'. What Christians should think,
repentantly, if they have taken to heart that they have a
Father in heaven, is 'How miserable to have let God down.'
To believe that God is wounded by the sins of God's
children is by no means to make light of sinfulness. The God
of the Christian faith is Someone who minds, not grim and

[16] *Showings*, chapters 22; 24; 77; see Tolley (2008).
[17] General Confession at Communion; see also epigraph to this chapter.

punitive but patient and resourceful. Indeed the Father image ought to come particularly into its own here.

The Gospel images of God as Father and God as King are both fundamental. They stand side by side supporting one another. When people are describing God's merciful dealings with human sinfulness, it is the Father image which is actually the more awesome of the two. Rulers may be lenient only because they are not troubled by their subjects' offences, or because they have calmly decided that clemency is the best policy. Maybe their hearts are somewhat touched by the joys and sorrows of their subjects. They may care about them as well as taking care of them. But this caring is hardly comparable with the way parents are concerned about what happens to their children, not just because they are kind people conscientiously doing their best, but directly for the sake of the beloved children themselves.

Of course human love is too uneven to be worthily compared with God's love. Some parents are lazy and irresponsible, or unfair, or selfishly absorbed in their own lives; and some are brutal. Not all parents use their imaginations. Some are so determined that their children shall be a credit to them that they treat them as appendages to the glory of the family. But the attention which children can expect of their parents, reasonably expect, is the kind of concern which goes beyond duty and is not reducible to justice. To affirm boldly that God's transcendent love is like this is to say that God goes beyond what fairness requires, because God is the heavenly Father and this is what God wants to do. God's children do not have to earn God's grace. As Julian heard God saying, 'Look how I loved you.'[18]

Further reading

Julian of Norwich (1978) *Showings*, Classics of western spirituality. Paulist Press.

Oppenheimer, Helen (2006) *What a piece of work*. Imprint Academic: Chapter 5 'Responding'.

Thompson, Marianne Meye (2000) *The promise of the Father*. Westminster John Knox Press.

---

[18] *Showings*, chapter 23.

Chapter 17

Divine Responsibility

This is very strange that GOD should Want. For in Him is
the Fulness of all Blessedness ...

Want in GOD is a Treasure to us. For had there been no
Need He would not have Created the World, nor made us,
nor Manifested His Wisdom, nor Exercised His Power, nor
Beautified Eternity, nor prepared the Joys of Heaven. But
He Wanted Angels and Men, Images, Companions.

Thomas Traherne, *Centuries*, I. 42

The main Christian image for God's love is the Father who
minds about his family; but, as usual, whatever one tries to
say about God, there is a 'both/and'. The ancient teaching
that God is without human passions[1] is not obsolete. Indeed
God's 'impassibility' has been much discussed in the last
few years.[2] Many faithful theologians believe that to imagine the heavenly Father as vulnerable like an earthly father
is not sound doctrine at all, but a mistake. They charge those
Christians who suppose that God suffers with falling into
sentimentality. It matters to heed this weighty tradition and
to attend to the concerns of both sides.

On the one hand, God is in control. God cannot be anxious or shaken, still less endangered or damaged, as if God's
wellbeing were at the mercy of God's creatures. A most
frightening idea for children is to realise that their parents
are upset. On the other hand, when people make too strong
a contrast between God's divine impassibility and human
sensitivity, their human reverence begins to look like insen-

---

[1]   See e.g. Article 1 of the 39 Articles of the Church of England.
[2]   See further reading list below and p. 136 above.

sitivity. Weighing intellectual arguments about whether one should suppose that God the Son suffered on the Cross, perhaps in one sense but not in another sense, verges on the kind of unfeeling indifference which Edwin Muir described as staring boldly at Christ's crucifixion.[3] This human and divine death was dreadful. The point of Incarnation was for God to enter compassionately into human experience.

To let in the positive 'both/and' of God transcending creation *and* minding about creation, the way has to be cleared by a 'neither/nor'. Christians cannot be content to think of God as Aristotle's Unmoved Mover,[4] the cause of everything, who remains untouched by everything. A blessedly aloof God on high who did not care about the suffering victims below would seem monstrous not holy. But nor must Christians proceed to reduce Almighty God to Whitehead's 'fellow-sufferer who understands',[5] who might be a gentle companion but could hardly be a strong Redeemer. There is scant encouragement in the idea that God is troubled like us, still less that eternal pain is built into God's being.[6] Christians who are inclined to give up 'impassibility' as dry and forbidding need to take care not to lose sight of God's unshakable safety. The Father to whom they pray is in heaven. Julian of Norwich 'saw him sitting' and was encouraged to believe that 'he dwells there eternally'.[7]

Somehow believers must hold on, like scientists struggling with the conflicting terminologies of waves and particles,[8] to the apparently contrary convictions, on the one hand that their holy God's security is infinite and invincible, and on the other hand that their loving God does mind. People who learn their faith from the Gospels may be encouraged to believe that the kindly prejudice is the less inadequate. Imagining God as a doting parent is less unworthy than imagining God as a heartless parent.

---

[3]   'Variations on a time theme IX' in Muir (1976).
[4]   *Metaphysics* XII. 7.
[5]   Whitehead (1978), p. 351.
[6]   See Gavrilyuk (2009), pp. 144–147.
[7]   *Showings*, e.g. chapter 68.
[8]   See above, pp. 33f, 137.

The positive affirmation which matters is that the Creator desired to make this world enough to bear its cost. Surely Julian's confidence was not heretical, that our courteous Lord[9] suffered gladly for our sake because 'We are his bliss'.[10] Nor was Traherne's wonder out of place, that God should want 'the Communication of His Divine Essence, and Persons to Enjoy it.'[11] For some of us, W. H. Vanstone's *God's endeavour, God's expense*[12] represented a breakthrough in responsible thinking about how making a universe is essentially arduous and the Creator takes pains with creation.

To speak of the Almighty as capable of distress is auda-cious picture-language, but surely the distinctive Christian message must incorporate this. Unless believers can say plainly that God minds, how can they affirm that 'God is love', in the face of all the evils of the world? It is all very well for people who emphasize that God is without pas-sions to state that God can know our hurts without feeling them, maintaining an 'epistemic distance'[13] between God and us, but that hardly amounts to good news. Does the Father held His children at arm's length? People who affirm God's impassibility may believe deeply in God's love but are likely to have difficulty in communicating this to other people.

Philosophical theology becomes desiccated unless it is well rooted in the naive story of how God's own Son came among us and experienced affliction. When Christians say that 'God was in Christ reconciling the world to himself',[14] they believe that the Passion of Christ revealed God's mind-ing. The Cross vindicates the faith that God is *present* though not *submerged* in human life, even when, particu-larly when, the experience of God's children is not happy but ghastly. The Resurrection comes in as the essential

---

[9]   *Showings*, e.g. chapter 77.
[10] ibid. e.g. chapter 22.
[11] Traherne (1960), I. 41; see also epigraph to this chapter.
[12] Vanstone (1977).
[13] Creel (1986), p. 129.
[14] *2 Corinthians* 5.19.

conclusion of this history, establishing not only God's right to create but God's power to restore.

This way of explaining the Atonement is an attempt to scotch a caricature. Christians sometimes envisage a blameless but vindictive God, ruling over human creatures who are all wretchedly sinful, some of them rebellious and some remorseful. This God is determined to punish somebody, and sends his Son to take our place and be punished for our sins. How could that help? Of course human beings are not guiltless, but surely the worst of them hardly deserve to be crucified. To suppose that justice can be established by torturing an innocent victim is not even ethical, still less a healing solution.

There are many puzzles about the meaning of the Cross, but it should be a help not a hindrance to hold on to the notion that the Holy Trinity, the Father, the Son and the Spirit, is united in concern for what human beings do and what happens to them.[15] Among the many efforts to expound the meaning of the Cross was the heresy called 'Patripassianism', which held that it was the Father who suffered. The Church rejected this account, because it confused the Father with the Son; but surely like most heresies it was trying to express a truth. If the Son suffers, it hardly makes sense to imagine the Father as blissfully untouched.[16] Whether in the ancient world, where a father ruled as sovereign over the family, or in the modern world, where parents are still in charge of their offspring's wellbeing, a parent cannot look on *impassively*, if that means indifferently, when a child is the one who is hurt.

Christians often sum up their belief in God's Atonement by announcing that Jesus Christ paid the price of sin. It is as important to affirm that he paid the price of evil. The idea that the creation was perfect until the rebellion of humanity 'brought death into the world and all our woe'[17] is mytho-

---

[15] See above, pp. 130f.
[16] cf. J. Moltmann: 'The Son suffers dying, the Father suffers the death of the Son. The grief of the Father here is just as important as the death of the Son', *The crucified God*, p. 243. See discussion in Castelo (2008).
[17] Milton, *Paradise lost* l.3.

logical. Christians preaching the Gospel ought not to put the whole blame upon human beings for all the troubles of life.[18] It was the God they worship who chose to make a world which was full of pain before human beings were born in it, where so many victims have always been more sinned against than sinning. One way of looking at the Cross is to consider with reverent gratitude that the Creator does not repudiate liability for the sufferings brought about by the making of a universe. Then, when the primary problem of evil has been acknowledged, that part of the problem which is the disobedience of beloved human creatures can take its proper place. God's generosity in paying the cost of creation includes taking responsibility for the sins of the whole world.

Sin comes almost at the beginning of the story; but first the Creator has seen that the universe, including humanity, is 'very good'. Hopeful followers of the Christian way are right to walk upright as people who are precious to one another and to God. They must still remember the converse fact that they are sinners with no merit of their own, whose only hope is God's mercy. They have to watch their step and keep on saying both / and.[19] People are not 'fairly satisfactory'. They are thoroughly valuable and thoroughly unworthy, and neither truth cancels the other. The argument always has to come back from the significance and sacredness of human beings to their selfishness and sinfulness, which need liberation rather than celebration.[20]

All human beings are complicit, variously, in the kinds of insensitivity, inertia and malice which have made the world the place where Jesus Christ suffered. It is seldom perfectly safe to say 'I am innocent of the blood of this just man.'[21] Penitent Christians are not being theatrical when they blame themselves for the Cross, because they realise that it could have been their fault. If they had been there themselves, they could easily have taken part with the people

---

[18] See Oppenheimer (2006, p. 115; 2001, e.g. pp. 16–18, 45, 114–115, 121).
[19] See above, pp. 71, 73.
[20] See above, p. 67.
[21] *Matthew* 27. 24.

who brought this savagery about, or at least with the ones who failed to do anything to stop it. They go to church on Good Friday to mourn the similar misdeeds they actually have committed, which are part of the weight of human badness. They are well assured that the God they worship is not set on punishing them. On the contrary, God wants to forgive them and put right what has gone wrong. The divine Judge 'desireth not the death of a sinner, but rather that he may turn from his wickedness, and live'.[22]

Christians who know that they are sinners believe that God will have mercy on them after all, because they keep hold of the conviction that the God who judges is indeed the heavenly Father, who positively wants to put everything right for his family. God is merciful, not from impersonal benevolence but as it were for God's own sake.[23] A critic might well say, 'How spoilt that child is!' That is what the elder brother of the prodigal son did say.[24] Parents whose reaction to bad behaviour is always 'Never mind: it doesn't matter,' let alone 'It's time for a party,' are not bringing up their children responsibly. In a way, the parable of the two sons is unfinished, waiting, precisely, for justification. The moral problem of Atonement is not, 'What can we do to placate our angry God?' but 'Is God's infinite mercy too cheap?'

How can the forgiveness which people need be morally validated? The question requires an answer, which Christian faith offers. The doctrine of the Atonement is not that the children were indulgently let off from their punishment, but that their heavenly Father took the responsibility for their going wrong. God's mercy on all the prodigals cannot be a superficial overlooking or condoning. God has to reckon with the gravity of sin, because God has chosen to create a world of people and they have done a great deal of damage. The way God has taken responsibility is by entering into human life and enduring the consequences of sin.

---

[22] *Book of Common Prayer*, Morning and Evening Prayer.
[23] See above, pp. 175–76.
[24] *Luke* 15. 11–32.

Christian attempts to explain Atonement and show how the Cross could be good news have not embroiled the Church in such bitter historical battles as their attempts to explain how God can be Three in One and how Christ can be divine and human. Whereas the doctrines of the Trinity and the Incarnation have been fixed, after much debate, in the creeds, there is no such definitive doctrine of the Atonement. There are theories and slogans offering to explain how the death of Jesus could make good the damage done by human sins, 'sufficient sacrifice' to satisfy holy wrath, 'penal substitution' of the innocent for the guilty, 'vicarious suffering' on our behalf, 'the perfect penitent' making amends ... but there is room to manoeuvre. If Christians could resist the constant temptation to unchurch one another, they could all be thankful to stand upon the bald statement that Christ died 'for us' and 'for our salvation' and fill this out with whichever explanations they find illuminating.

The difficult practical processes of forgiving and being forgiven do not have to be summed up in one formula or recipe. What all the Christian theories about the Cross are trying to say is that God does not give sinners up for lost. What has gone wrong with human life is agonizing but not finally fatal.

One attempt to understand the meaning of Atonement is the idea that it takes a sacrifice to make amends for sins. First century believers, both Jewish and pagan, who were tying to make sense of the Cross were used to the practice of worshipping God by offering up something of real value. They could accordingly explain the death of Jesus Christ as one kind of sacrifice, a sin-offering: indeed as *the* sin-offering, which paid for the sins of the whole world.[25] The moral point which this interpretation of the Atonement grasps is that on the first Good Friday God did something decisive. The Cross of Christ really is more *crucial* than a sort of visual aid which may help us to see how much God loves us.

---

[25] *Book of Common Prayer*, Holy Communion: Prayer of Consecration.

God's mercy is harshly challenged by the valid moral claim that to ignore sin without more ado would impugn God's holiness, because sin is indeed intolerable. The belief that there must be a price to pay for wrongdoing is not merely a primitive superstition; though rational moralists may well be doubtful about some of the ways human beings have set about paying that price and making peace with their gods.

Christians have found predictions of God's reconciliation with humanity in their ancient scriptures. They have dared to seize upon the primitive tale of Abraham's willingness to offer up his beloved only son Isaac,[26] finding positive hopeful meaning in this as an image of God's own sacrifice. The significance Christians have drawn from the old story is that Abraham's obedience and God's provision of a substitute victim pointed towards the perfect and complete sin-offering which was to come, when the sacrifice would be neither Isaac nor a poor ram caught in a bush, but God's own beloved Son offering himself.

Christians who want to build upon this assurance should be more careful not to confuse Calvary with Tophet, the dread place where parents offered up their children to the god Moloch. For Abraham and Isaac the savage ending is averted at the last moment; but the story still appears shocking, even offensive, not because the very idea of sacrifice is now obsolete, but because it does not seem to matter what Isaac the chosen victim felt about his binding.

Whether or not Christians find the terminology of sacrifice as sin-offering intelligible, they can take the narrative of Abraham's ordeal as an parable recounting God's readiness to pay any price. God the Father is willing even to give up his Son and God the Son is willing even to give up his life. What justifies believers in giving the old story this interpretation? The necessary historical assurance that the faithfulness of God is no fantasy of the imagination is the life, death and rising of Christ. Jesus of Nazareth was a real human being, whose followers have come to believe that he is the

---

[26] *Genesis* 22.

unique Son of God, God made human. This individual man did pay a fearful price and vindicated Christian faith in his divine authority by rising from the dead.

Accordingly to this understanding, what the Atonement means is that God the Son could and did fully represent God the Father in taking the responsibility for human wickedness and so validating divine mercy and justifying divine forgiveness. The parable of the father's dealings with his two sons[27] has come true, except that this elder brother is at one with his father and has himself put into effect the very same purpose, to welcome the prodigal home.

For the divine mercy to be authentic, it was morally necessary for the Creator, who has placed people in this world, to experience what life in this world is like, to live in a human body and suffer literally, not metaphorically, to make amends for everything that has gone wrong with the creation. The Son in the name of the Father felt the reality of sin, undergoing at first hand the damage God's children do. This is a possible way to make ethical sense of the apparently immoral doctrine of penal satisfaction. The notion that God is 'satisfied' by punishing Jesus instead of us would appear positively unjust if it put the whole emphasis on God the righteous Judge, hiding God the responsible Father who is ready to meet the outstanding cost of the children's wrongdoing.

The doctrine that God's purpose is atonement still has to have a more judicial aspect. It could still be facile to say that the Cross demonstrates how God's children hurt their Father terribly but their Father loves and forgives them none the less. If that were all, the Atonement would be all very well for sinners but would hardly take account of the harm they have done. Wronged human beings would have the right to call God's mercy shallow or even unethical.

Kind parents are not impartial judges of the way their family behave. Parents are naturally inclined to forgive their own children whatever they do; but they are open to charges of irresponsibility and injustice when they try to

---

[27] See above, pp. 166, 182.

keep the problem hidden in the family and ignore the damage their offspring keep doing to other people. Recent events have shown the horrible results of Christians falling into this very error, trying to protect their church's reputation by condoning the abuse of children by Christian priests.

Christian moralists affirm the principle that all sins are sins against God and therefore God alone can judge; but meanwhile innocent human beings are being hurt all the time and feel for themselves the unfairness of superficial mercy. The people who have been ill-treated have a good right to be indignant if the offenders are pardoned unpunished. How can a just God up on high set aside unrighted wrongs and take credit for being generous to the wrongdoers?

The Hebrew Bible may seem more realistic about justice than the New Testament. Christians are shocked when they realise that the scriptures include pious cries to God not to forgive sinners but to take revenge on behalf of oppressed people. About a third of the psalmists feel themselves beset by enemies. They are inclined to imagine savage retribution with vivid ferocity.[28] In the beloved Psalm 23, God's flock enjoy their well-protected feeding all the better in the envious presence of their foes. Psalm 143 concludes, 'And of thy goodness slay mine enemies', as an evidently reasonable request. Of course Christians want to dissociate themselves from all this. The cursing psalms are usually not sung, and the detachable embarrassing verses are omitted. The problem remains, because the self-righteous psalmists had a valid ethical point to make. If moralists who disapprove of their rancour proceed to reduce God's mercy without more ado to meekness and mildness, God's justice goes by default.

Christians accept that resentment is forbidden and so they may underestimate the outstanding moral problem of atonement. They hardly think that it really matters if guilty people get off scot-free. On the contrary, that is just what

[28] e.g. *Psalms* 3; 18; 140.

they hope will happen, because they have learnt to count themselves among the guilty people who need clemency. They are not allowed to be identified with the righteous ones who are crying out for God to redress their wrongs, but always have to count themselves among the unrighteous who have committed the wrongs.

Far from longing for justice as vindication, sinners are bound to be fearful of justice as punishment. They cannot expect a verdict of Not Guilty, but they may plead for a merciful sentence. They thankfully believe that all will be well for them, because the Son of God takes the part of miserable sinners and reconciles them to the Father. It is not too difficult to feel forgiven. 'God will pardon me, it is His trade' said Heinrich Heine on his deathbed.[29] But there is a missing link. Does God have the moral right to be the friend of sinners and side with the wrongdoers? If a judge sets aside the law and kindly lets the culprits go free, that is injustice, especially if the culprits are members of his family. It is victims who have the right to forgive and who can agree to be reconciled.

Therefore the story of the reconciliation of God and humanity needs completion by the story of the Passion. It is not enough to say that God the Son represents the kind Father who will not punish sinners but is on their side and goes on loving them however little they deserve any mercy. God's judgment must also take notice of the people who are sinned against, who have been ill-treated for no blame of their own. The crucified Lord literally became one of these, not merely looking down pitifully from above but directly representing the people whose afflictions are other people's fault. When God came into the world as a human being, God became one of the victims, who had real hurts to forgive and who therefore had the recognizable authority to make peace.

The doctrine of the Atonement affirms that the God who died and rose again has both divine and human authority to choose forgiveness rather than vengeance. On the one hand,

[29] 'Dieu me pardonnera, c'est son métier' *Oxford dictionary of quotations*, Fifth edition, 'Last words', p. 455:9.

Jesus Christ as Son of God represents his Father, who does not feebly ignore or condone the misdoings of his children but takes responsibility for the whole family. On the other hand, Jesus Christ as Son of Man himself becomes one of the hurt people whose wrongs cry out for justice. In his human living and dying he becomes the representative of them all and so has the right to forgive the enemies who have done this harm.

The belief that the Cross somehow 'makes satisfaction' and endorses God's mercy on the sins of the whole world must be based on a robust understanding of what this notion of a representative can mean. Does it really make sense for somebody to stand in for someone else and take over someone else's responsibility? Theologians do their best to explain. If they are not to be glib or presumptuous, they need to learn from people who have first-hand experience of real enmity. Christians must be willing to consider whether this idea of God the Son making amends *on behalf* of sinners for the wrongs they have done to their victims is morally strong enough to take the weight.

At least this kind of doctrine of atonement need not leave commonsense behind and take off into indistinct theorizing. The questions to be answered are moral and practical questions about who has the right and the authority to be a representative. The idea of one person representing another is not darkly mysterious. It is an ordinary and useful notion. Human beings often do things on one another's behalf. They characteristically know what it means to take someone else's place or to act for someone else's sake. The wonder of the God they worship taking the place of sinners to make atonement for their sake does not have to be intellectually baffling; but it is, indeed, 'amazing grace'.

The God of Christian faith is the God who reckons with what it is like to be a human creature, 'first hand, as one of us'.[30] When Christians try to give reason for the exacting faith which is in them,[31] they do not have to submit their moral and intellectual integrity to the arbitrary sovereignty

[30] Weinandy (2000), p. 206.
[31] *1 Peter* 3.15.

of a tyrannical Ruler of the universe. They have glimpses of a God who took the risk[32] of making this world with all its inhabitants, in order to bring them through struggles to fulfilment. The blameless but vindictive Almighty is replaced by the responsible and resourceful Creator, who has taken full unlimited responsibility for what has gone wrong, for the sake of the final outcome. For people who are haunted by the question whether the Creator can be good when the creation is so troubled, this is the necessary beginning of an answer

Further reading

Castelo, Daniel (2008) 'Moltmann's dismissal of divine impassibility' *Scottish journal of theology* 2008:4.

Castelo, Daniel (2009) *The apathetic God: exploring the contemporary relevance of divine impassibility*. Paternoster Theological Monographs

Creel, Richard E. (1986) *Divine impassibility: An essay in philosophical theology*. Cambridge University Press.

Creel, Richard E.(1997) 'Immutability and impassibility' in *A companion to philosophy of religion*. Blackwell. (In which he records a significant change of mind, affirming that 'God is touched by our joys and sorrows.')

Fiddes, Paul (1988) *The creative suffering of God* 1988 Clarendon paperbacks.

Fiddes, Paul (2001) 'Creation out of love' in Polkinghorne (below).

Gavrilyuk, Paul L. (2004) *The suffering of the impassible God*. Oxford Early Christian Studies.

Gavrilyuk, Paul L. (2009) 'God's impassible suffering in the flesh' in Keating & White (below).

Julian of Norwich (1978) *Showings*, Classics of western spirituality. Paulist Press.

Keating, James F. and Thomas Joseph White, ed. (2009) *Divine impassibility and the mystery of human suffering*. Eerdmann.

Oppenheimer, Helen (2001) *Making good*. SCM Press: especially Chapter 7 'Wanting'.

Polkinghorne, John, ed. (2001) *The work of love: creation as kenosis*. SPCK.

Traherne, Thomas (1960) *Centuries* . Faith Press.

Vanstone, W.H. (1977) *God's endeavour, God's expense*. DLT.

Weinandy, Thomas G. (2000) *Does God suffer?* T & T Clark.

---

[32]   See e.g. Arthur Peacocke in Polkinghorne (2001), p. 40.

Chapter 18

Human Responsibility

> … hear thou in heaven thy dwelling place; and when thou hearest, forgive.

> *2 Chronicles* 6.21 (Solomon's prayer)

Christians believe that God the Creator made amends for the sins of the whole world. They often express this by saying that God the Son represented sinful humanity and took their due punishment. These are statements about law and justice, fairness and unfairness. The promise that God and sinners are to be reconciled is more than this.[1] The mercy of God which brings the sinners home and restores them to their place in the family cannot be confined to legal technicalities about how the penalty has been paid on their behalf and therefore their Advocate in heaven has persuaded the Judge to commute their sentence. For children of God, the positive mending of broken relationships with God and one another means more than accurately balancing the heavenly books and making sure that punishments and rewards are fairly allocated.[2] The meaning of the word *atonement* is indeed 'at-one-ment'.

The mending of damaged goodwill goes beyond measuring people's just deserts and even goes beyond mercifully consenting to give sinners another chance. Christians have not always entered wholeheartedly into what this *going beyond* ought to mean. Followers of Jesus have lost sight of his overriding faith in the generous Father. Some of them

---

[1]   See Oppenheimer (2006), chapter 16, 'Forgiving'. That chapter was itself based upon a University Sermon I preached in Cambridge in 1983, called 'Grievances', which was printed in *Theology* January 1988.

[2]   See above, p. 166f.

have stayed fixed in legal correctness. They have heard his vivid warnings that people who reject love are on the way to destruction and have proceeded to build the fear of God's Wrath into the foundation of unloving penal theories about God's dealings with sinners. The Lord's image of the refuse smouldering and decaying in the Jerusalem rubbish-dump called Gehenna[3] has been developed into realistic portrayals of Hell in words or paint as a grisly torture-chamber where immortal fellow-sinners are to be imprisoned and punished eternally for their outstanding offences. Enthusiastic relish for the threat of divine retribution always hanging over the heads of God's recalcitrant subjects has sometimes been only too characteristic of Christian piety. Edwin Muir is almost a lone voice yearning for even Judas the traitor to come home and be forgiven at last.[4]

Paul the Pharisee, whose particular vocation turned out to be bringing the good news of God's mercy to the Gentiles, wrestled with the question of reconciliation at the centre of the Christian faith. It was too clear that Jesus Christ had died because the Jewish leaders had handed him over to the Romans. Had God's ancient people forfeited their promised place in the Kingdom when they rejected their Messiah? Paul gave the answer 'God forbid.'[5] He was convinced that God could and would graft the olive branch back into the tree, so that all Israel would be saved.[6] Is his theology of heavenly mercy more convincing than his arboriculture? The succeeding history of the Gentiles and the Jews makes a sorry story. When cruelty does not corrupt, condescension does. The old Prayer Book collect for Good Friday, which should have been an opportunity for Christians to pray humbly and hopefully for all the estranged members of God's family, has given much more offence than encouragement to 'Jews, Turks, Infidels, and Hereticks'. Its redrafting to express unpretentious goodwill is not being found easy.

---

[3] e.g. *Mark* 9.43–44.
[4] 'The Transfiguration' in Muir (1960).
[5] *Romans* 11.1 (King James Bible translation; lit. 'Let it not be.')
[6] *Romans* 11. 23, 26.

Now that the world has seen the horrors of Hitler's fascism, Christians have come to realise more clearly where careless anti-Semitism has led. It is high time for them to realise that the conflict, which goes right back to the beginning of the church, has been a tragic family quarrel among the children of Abraham. Generations of Jews have suffered from the inclusion in the Passion story of the terrible curse, 'His blood be on us and on our children.'[7] It is as if the serpent, being trampled underfoot, achieved a potent dying sting to hurt God's people. Meanwhile Zechariah's prophecy seems unfulfilled: 'In those days ten men from the nations of every tongue shall take hold of the robe of a Jew, saying, "Let us go with you, for we have heard that God is with you."'[8] Christians ought to learn to enter gratefully into their Jewish heritage, rather than simply confiscating the parts of it they want for themselves.

The Christian faith is founded upon the idea of reconciliation, which would be meaningless if it were not practical. Who can put it into practice? Who has authority to make peace between old enemies, to cancel old injuries and to do better than either punishing or condoning? A judge's role is to decide whether or not there is reason to remit a penalty, or to determine that there is no case to answer. In special circumstances, a guilty prisoner may be lawfully released on compassionate grounds. What nobody can do in a legal capacity is forgive. Offering judicial forgiveness is too much like offering an insult to the victims of the offence.

The Christian doctrine of atonement seems to mean that the judge has gone further than legally acquitting the offender and has submitted to be punished himself. Is justice satisfied by this substitution? The problem is not that the idea of people taking other people's places and representing them is incoherent or even difficult in itself. It happens all the time in human life. The problem is that for representation to work there has to be a proper mandate. Making free with other people's responsibilities without

---

[7]   *Matthew* 27.25.
[8]   *Zechariah* 8.23.

permission may be an intrusion not unlike making free with other people's purses.

The question-mark against the notion of repenting of sins which are not one's own emerged noticeably with the centenary celebrations of the abolition of the slave trade. Admissions of guilt were called for, but the people who were responsible for the miseries of slavery are long since dead. People today can hardly judge how sinful or excusable individuals may have been, still less presume to take the responsibility of apologizing to the descendants of the slaves in the name of long-ago offenders.

What form can my disowning of historical sins take? With whom in the past should I, can I, identify? How much of my present comfort is disgraceful because I owe it to my ancestors' misdoings? Some of us are better off now because the slave-trade was profitable. I feel confident that I need not repent of being a slave-trader, but it seems to make sense to say that the person I am might have been content to benefit from the trade, or have been a slave-owner. Would the upbringing and education I would have had then exonerate me from blame? Would I, alive then, have innocently or culpably taken the situation for granted, or uneasily tried to suppress guilty feelings? May I align myself with Wilberforce, or anyway not feel ashamed but hold my head up, because I am glad to belong to the nation which did put a stop to the abomination? These questions are unanswerable, not just hard to answer. I was not there in the past to do anything for blame or credit. I have a complete alibi for the time when the crimes happened. However adequately or inadequately I am living up to the responsibilities I have now, I can have duties only to individuals whose lives can somehow or other be linked with mine, so that what I do now makes some difference to them, whether I realise this or not

For believers, all human beings are children of God and all their lives are linked.[9] Though people have to start where they are with real duties and not allow themselves to

---

[9]   See above, Chapter 13.

wander, however amiably, in imaginary worlds, they cannot always predict where and how far their journeys in the real world will take them. The answer to 'Am I my brother's keeper?',[10] once I ask the question, is apt to be 'Yes.' People who take to heart the idea of moral responsibility for one another must desist from looking on themselves as unattached atoms with the right, if they wish, to be contentedly separate.[11] The miller who sang, 'I care for nobody, no not I, And nobody cares for me' may have been a jolly miller, but if he meant what he sang his humanity was sadly diminished.

Christians affirm that human lives are linked because Jesus Christ was God with us and died for us all.[12] If they take this to heart and say readily, 'We killed him', that could be as superficial as twenty-first century people claiming responsibility for the slave trade. The theology of the Cross is more realistic than shifting blame around. One of its meanings is that the Creator who made the world entered into the web of responsibilities which is human history.[13] Jesus the Son of God was willing to die as a representative of all the victims of everybody's sins. He suffered then because cruelty and bigotry, carelessness and feebleness, were, as they still are, persistently characteristic of human beings.

Nobody except the God who made the world and came to live in it could make amends like this for the troubles of the world. That is what the uniqueness of Christ means. Too often Christians seem to be saying, 'Our Saviour is bigger and better than yours.' Sometimes they seem to be telling unhappy people that because Jesus Christ has made amends their dreadful troubles really do not matter and all they need is faith in God. What a Christian should be saying is, 'I have been told about a God who faced the troubles of the world. That is the God I can worship.'

---

[10]   *Genesis* 4.9.
[11]   See above, pp. 15, 70–71, 91.
[12]   e.g. *Romans* 5.8; *2 Corinthians* 5.19; *Philippians* 2.5–8.
[13]   See above, pp. 179–83.

The actual crucifixion of Jesus was no legend or myth. It happened in history. We who are alive now were in no way part of that particular man's story. But because we behave now in the manifold unacceptable ways which made it happen then, we cannot wash our hands of blame for what this world is still like. It is realistic for Christian teaching to begin with 'Repent'.[14]

Agnostic humanists may be happy to agree with Christians that human beings are not unconnected atoms, but they may still not be happy about where the argument has been going. However naturally congenial the belief that we are all bound in one bundle may be to people who count themselves as humane, the idea that this bundle is a mass of perdition will be much less congenial. Even friendly outsiders are repelled by what they see as the Christian obsession with sin. They soon lose patience with people who are endlessly meek and mild, who take the blame for everything and refuse ever to stand up for themselves.[15] Doormats do not make good role models.

This is a powerful indictment of Christian ethics. Believers who receive it as fair criticism and are willing to learn from it may realise that it can be more Christian to be less sure about guilt. Sometimes offences can be managed and hurts allowed to heal, without always making such a fuss. Christians could take more heed of their own teaching that in God's sight they are children. They need not always be so anxious about their own or other people's moral status. They might remember the duellist in a poem by Browning, who bitterly wished that he and the enemy he had just killed could be boys again, who could handle wrongs without needing to fight to the death.[16]

Although children often have to say 'sorry', they are not taught to wallow in self-abnegation. There is something wrong with a child that 'o'er its own shortcomings weeps

---

[14]   *Mark* 1.15.
[15]   See Oppenheimer (2006), p. 119.
[16]   Robert Browning, 'After'.

with loathing.'[17] It is not depravity, let alone total depravity, that puts everyday pressure on parents, but heedlessness, tantrums and whining. Miserable remorse is not what the adults require to atone for naughtiness. As John Keats realized, mawkish emotion is an adolescent aberration, characteristic neither of childhood nor of maturity.[18] Even the prodigal son who had wasted his inheritance was not required to do penance for his selfish irresponsibility. What he had to do was get up and go home, where he found his Father coming out joyfully to meet him.[19]

Self-centred remorse is unconstructive and gives Christian morality a bad name. Are Christians who want to be good not only dismal but characteristically hypocritical and manipulative? When there is a great deal of guilt about, virtuous people too easily maintain their own valued good standing by freely acknowledging how bad they are, thereby letting much of their blame run off on to other people who are not so worried about being good or bad. My repentance does me credit and puts you in the wrong for being angry with me. This is not justification by faith but justification by twisted humility. The targets of this tactic would be well advised to refuse to join in the to-and-fro game of competitive blame-taking. They could allow the self-confessed sinners to go on glorying in their shame and feeling as guilty as they seem to wish. Self-denigration is apt to be quite judgmental. It is no way to achieve real reconciliation between faulty but not really malicious people, who would do better to put their differences behind them and behave like normal responsive human beings.

There is a frightening tendency towards masochism in some Christian piety and believers need to be more careful not to give colour to this charge. There are aspects of Christian history which positively invite the accusation that the 'good news' is packed with torments and tortures, mental and physical, often self-imposed. To rational outsiders,

---

[17] R. F. Littledale (tr.) 'Come down, O Love Divine' *Hymns ancient and modern* no. 670.

[18] John Keats, Preface to *Endymion*.

[19] See above, p. 166.

miserable sinners simply appear unhealthy, rather than properly human. Penance looks maudlin, hairshirts unwholesome and beautifully fashioned crucifixes practically pornographic.

The Gospels themselves show a marked restraint in their unemotional, almost deadpan, Good Friday narratives. Christians ought to remember that, far from welcoming martyrdom, the Lord prayed in dismay that the cup might pass. His followers have to be ready to take up their own crosses, but they should still understand that not all adversities are crosses which people ought to bear. It was more characteristic of Jesus to set about making people well than to instruct them to endure their afflictions. The Cross would mean less if the welcome works of healing had not first shown what human life ought to be like. It is strange that people to whom 'salvation' is so important should miss its basic meaning of 'health'.

It has taken feminists to notice how masochistic the Church sometimes allows itself to become. Christian men have found it too easy to apply the Gospel ideal of meekness one-sidedly and unkindly, to reinforce traditional human assumptions about gender. It has seemed thoroughly Christian to encourage women to submit to ill-treatment and even to rejoice at the privilege of undeserved suffering.[20] Modesty has demanded that girls, unlike boys, should be taught not to stand up for themselves. Christians are coming belatedly to realize that women are children of God as much as men, but the lesson they have absorbed is to hold up the 'womanly' virtue of humbleness as an example for men to follow too. They have not learnt so well to hold up 'manly' courageous energy as a quality to be encouraged in women.

Humanists credibly accuse Christians of being uncharitably engrossed by sinfulness, but their own attitudes are not always more generous. The human tendency to look for faulty culprits to be responsible for every ill is not an especially religious mistake. Unbelievers are as much involved

---

[20]   See e.g. VandenBerg (2007) for a thoughtful response to the criticism that Christianity glorifies suffering.

as believers in what is now being called our 'culture of blame'. A contentious liking for litigation comes naturally to indignant human beings, who would like to think of themselves as too civilised to be vengeful, but who still feel deep down that any bad treatment they are getting demands recognition as outstandingly important.

What is an especially religious mistake is the idea that wherever there is blame the proper way to deal with it is to cancel it out of hand. Christians who have become horrified by the idea of eternal punishment tip the moral balance so far the other way that they preach a feeble Gospel of a lenient God who is content for people to get away with anything. The facile distortion of Christian ethics that has nothing more constructive to offer to offenders than a knee-jerk 'I forgive them' does wobble on the brink of hypocrisy.

Overlooking bad behaviour is not only dangerously unjust to the innocent. It may be unfair to the sinners. Mercy can appear as more insulting than generous, if the culprit's integrity is not allowed to matter. Offenders who accept their own blame and want to do something towards paying their moral debts are not being masochistic.

Because getting forgiveness right is central to the Gospel, this matter of the sinner's integrity is worth illustrating with a narrative. A. D. Nuttall in his attractive book *Shakespeare the thinker* describes *Measure for measure* as Shakespeare's 'most daring essay on the relation between ethics and theology'.[21] His exploration of the way wrongdoing is handled in that play sheds light, not only on Shakespeare's drama, but on the ethical questions about atonement and blame which Shakespeare opens up. Shakespeare's characters are people we know, with the difference that we may make critical judgements on their lives without being intrusive or impertinent.

Angelo's fall and restoration could provide, not so much a case study balancing the pros and cons of an ethical problem, as a kind of parable like a Gospel parable, which illuminates moral meaning by bringing out a particular ethical

[21] Nuttall (2007), p. 274.

point. The once-priggish now disgraced Angelo does not ask to escape his punishment. He asks only to save the remnants of his honour by undergoing the death he knows he deserves. Nuttall notices that the conclusion in which he is let off refuses him the grace of being taken at his word: 'his request is benevolently / insultingly denied.'[22] Generosity is less simple and mercy is less manageable than easy-going Christians suppose. Is the play's happy ending embellished with marriage vows therefore tarnished?

It is fair to bear in mind that the terms of reference of a Jacobean play, presented not as a tragedy but as a comedy, are that forgiveness followed by weddings can rightly be taken as a properly satisfying conclusion. That would be what the audience would understand when the characters pair off at the end. Was it, as Nuttall suggests, Shakespeare's successful subversive intention to cast doubt on this conclusion and leave a purposely uncomfortable outcome? Or does the discomfort which remains come from a failure in this play, because Shakespeare has intended a happy ending but not contrived to give it enough practical moral substance to make it convincing?

A theologian cannot help wanting to try to follow up the parable, not rejecting Nuttall's moral discernment but accepting his insight and then going on to suggest that the ambivalence which has changed mercy into an insult need not be accepted as the final outcome. Sequels to masterpieces seldom come off, but one may be permitted to wonder if a novelist could take up the story of Angelo and Mariana and consider how on such a flimsy practical basis this damaged man and this hurt woman could gently piece their lives together. Could their unpropitious union turn out, not exactly as a happy ending, but possibly as a happy beginning? Once the sinner's integrity has been seriously recognized, perhaps clemency need not be permanently denied its happy upshot, but promised its fulfilment in the generous restoration of goodwill.

---

[22] ibid.

Shakespeare's story firmly stops, but not without giving the hopeful interpretation a little more backing than Nuttall suggests. Shakespeare makes it completely clear that Angelo's condemnation could not be lifted by a perfunctory cancellation of his offence. His pardon would be contrary to justice, except that it is positively validated by a huge piece of moral luck.[23] Angelo is not in fact guilty of judicial murder. Claudio has not been executed and when he reappears alive, 'By this Lord Angelo perceives he's safe.'[24] The Duke who has to judge him recognizes 'a quickening in his eye', indicating that he can now after all be glad not affronted at being freed. Pardon really is mercy not insult. Having honestly faced his guilt, Angelo is capable now of emerging from the nightmare. This gleam of hope is what makes the story relevant to the Christian doctrine of atonement.

The happy ending which *Measure for measure* only sketches can be fairly welcomed as a moral ending characteristic of Shakespearean ethics. Angelo need not die 'for Claudio's death'[25] because Claudio is not dead. What his reconciliation needs is the endorsement of the women he really has wronged, the spontaneous forgiveness of Mariana and the struggling forgiveness of Isabella. A producer hoping to convey all this to an audience might well say to the actors, 'It lies much in your holding up'.[26]

Human beings can be ministers of grace and take part in redeeming one another. Reconciliation has a foothold in human nature. Christians may be able to illuminate their faith in the ultimate mercy of God by looking at human mercy as an image of what God's forgiveness might be like. Sometimes human mercy is heroic, when victims forgive terrorists and torturers. Most Christians can only hope that in such a situation they would find and show the needful grace. In ordinary life, forgiveness is apt to take the form of patience, no high drama but a willingness to go on quietly and slowly, a steady recognition that sinners are people and

---

[23] See Williams (1961).
[24] *Measure for measure*, V. i. 490.
[25] ibid. line 440.
[26] ibid. Scene 3, line 1.

that people are sinners, a creative readiness to be encouraged, an assurance that damaging wrongs can metamorphose into tales of long ago.

God's people would be wise not to base their moral lives on gloomily legalistic preconceptions about how totally blameworthy everyone is in God's sight. Finite and precarious though human value is, what God has created is not a sham. We can hope to recognize human glory and to be able to compare it with the brightness of our modest-sized sun and its planets among the galaxies, or more accurately with the lovely reflected brilliance of the moon.

On the one hand, human disobedience which needs God's mercy is only too real. The Fatherhood of God has to mean more than kind indulgence, because it requires God's unflagging purpose to set human life to rights, however great the challenge. The necessary pledge of that intent is the Cross, in the light of the Resurrection. The human death of the Son of God and his triumphant rising are both essential, to establish both God's will and God's power to make good. Evils are not to be ignored nor even cancelled but engulfed, to become part of a whole the more excellent for having cost so much.

On the other hand, the actual bad behaviour of God's children which needs atonement is not even now the whole truth about the human family. Human moral understanding need not be written off as simply invalid, nor honour as merely illusory, nor promise as wholly unrealistic. Human wisdom really is marvellous, like the marvel of a small child's first moral insights. People's achievements really are excellent, like the naive works of art made in nursery schools. Surely the heavenly Father is pleased, we may dare to imagine moved with joy, at the children's enthusiastic efforts and the progress they are making. St Gregory of Nyssa suggested that 'the perfection of human nature consists perhaps in its very growth in goodness'.[27]

If the Christian faith is true, human creatures and their doings matter in the whole scheme of things. God's creation

---

[27]   *Life of Moses*, Prologue, 10.

is not aimless doodling. God has struggled to realise a huge masterpiece still more precious than *Hamlet* or Beethoven's violin concerto or Michelangelo's Sistine ceiling.[28] God's mighty work of art is made up of living people, every one of whom is somebody, with complicated needs and aspirations, all related to one another and to their Maker in an expanding network of responsiveness. All the more-or-less legalistic things moralists want to say about human credit and human blame are overwhelmed by the active generosity of the Father Almighty.

Further reading

Nuttall, A.D. (2007) *Shakespeare the thinker*. Yale University Press; and Shakespeare's *Measure for measure* Act 5

Oppenheimer, Helen (1995) 'Remembering', *Theology* November/December.

Oppenheimer, Helen (2001) *Making good*. SCM Press.

Oppenheimer, Helen (2006) *What a piece of work*. Imprint Academic: Chapter 16 'Forgiving'

Williams, Bernard (1961) 'Moral luck,' *Proceedings of the Aristotelian Society* Supplementary Vol. L (Reprinted in *Moral luck: Philosophical papers 1973–1980* Cambridge University Press).

---

[28]   See Oppenheimer (2001), e.g. pp. 39–40.

Chapter 19

Welcome

'You must sit down,' says Love, 'and taste my meat.'
So I did sit and eat.

George Herbert 'Love bade me welcome'

Nobody could think of God's masterpiece as already per-
fected. All human lives are faulty and the happiest of them
remain vulnerable to trouble and distress. Every human
being who has not yet died is going to die. Optimism is
honourable but has to await fulfilment.

Christian optimism affirms that someone's life story is
not ended with the part we can see.[1] Believers make claims
about eternity, which they back up with arguments. Their
most convincing arguments are based upon testimony: that
is, on what human beings have seen and heard. Religious
faith is commonly based upon trusting other people to tell
truly what they have learned and how they have come to
where they are.[2]

People who affirm that there is indeed a God who has
made the universe and is bringing it to fulfilment are bound
to be asked how this God can be found. Some people have a
plain answer, that God has spoken to them. If this never
happened, faith could hardly get started. In that case sceptics would have reason to set aside all religions as human
wishful thinking.

Believers should not expect that messages suddenly
arriving, addressed to individuals as clear calls coming
directly from on high, will be anything but exceptional. The

---

[1]   See Oppenheimer (1988).
[2]   See above, p. 128.

way people more often approach God is like the way they meet other people, by being introduced. Christians have generally been introduced to God through the Church and through the Bible, that is to say, through people who have become acquainted with God already. Many would-be believers are not sure whether they can say for themselves that they know God yet. They would not claim to be on the same footing as the people who introduced them, although they hope that a happy relationship is beginning to develop.

A large objection appears. It is all very well to set different images of God side by side and learn from them all; but is this image of a stranger we hope to meet actually compatible with the more basic image of God as our loving Father, or does it undercut and destroy it? Is it responsible to accept the invitation in the Gospels to put our full trust in Someone we are still hoping to encounter? There are human fathers indeed who are more like strangers, fathers who are remote from their children for good and bad reasons, overworked fathers, uncaring fathers, absent fathers, but these cannot help anyone to believe in a heavenly Father who loves His children.

Christians who have the particular vocation to commend their faith to sceptics are obliged to make more effort to integrate the stories they are telling, in order to build up a consistent picture. The idea that we need to find God and the idea that we can come to know God as our Father can be reconciled by taking hold of the emphasis which mattered to St Paul. Christians believe that God is the Father of our Lord Jesus Christ, who has accepted human beings by adoption and grace as children and heirs.[3] This may look like a legalistic development of the trustful faith that Christ taught, but it could hearten some believers who need help for their unbelief.[4] There are people whose Christian experience is like being a wanted child, brought up by parents who have always been there; but there are many children of God in sophisticated societies who find themselves more in

---

[3]   *Romans* 8.15; *Galatians* 4.5; *Ephesians* 1.5; *Book of Common Prayer*, Collect for Christmas day.

[4]   *Mark* 9.24.

the situation of adopted older children, who have to learn to belong to their new families.

The Gospel of resurrection is that people's relationships with God and one another, begun on earth, are meant to last after death. What this signifies evidently goes beyond present human experience. The meaning of heaven cannot be pinned down in prosaic speech but may be none the worse for that. Ordinary reality often needs more than literal expression to do it justice.[5] Even for people's everyday communications, it is not an unnecessary luxury to rely upon imagery for conveying deeper meaning.

Human beings have found many images, both profound and light-hearted, for their hopes of eternal life. We shall wake up in a different world. St Peter will open the pearly gates and let us in to kneel before God's throne. We shall lie down in green pastures, beside still waters.[6] We shall be guests eating and drinking at a heavenly feast. We shall take our places in the angelic choir. For many people music is the most sublime of the arts and music-making the most satisfying image for a life occupied with the praise of God. There is no need to be condescending about traditional harps nor to phase them out as if they were old-fashioned or sentimental, though they are not the only instruments suitable for holy melodies.

C. S. Lewis suggested a more unexpected but persuasive image of eternal life. He defended the human hope of 'glory'.[7] He argued that since it is good children, not naughty children, who are eager for grown–up praise, it may be an important aspect of heaven that this innocent wish is to be fulfilled, that human beings shall actually know at last that they have really pleased the One they were created to please. His idea expresses St Paul's expectation that when the Lord discloses the purposes of the heart, 'each one will receive commendation from God'.[8]

---

[5]   See above, p. 127.
[6]   Psalm 23.2.
[7]   'The weight of glory' Sermon printed in Lewis (1962), pp. 204–205.
[8]   *1 Corinthians* 4.5.

It has been said that the Bible begins in a garden and ends in a city. Both these images have provided pictures of what the delights of Paradise could be like. People find heavenly satisfaction in tending their earthly gardens, co-operating with nature to bring something beautiful into existence.

> So we, in godlike mood,
> May of our love create our earth
> And see that it is good.[9]

By no means contradicting this rural image, the Book of Revelation describes God's city in a happily definite word-picture: 'Then he showed me the river of the water of life, bright as crystal, flowing from the throne of God and of the Lamb through the middle of the street of the city; also, on either side of the river, the tree of life with its twelve kinds of fruit, yielding its fruit each month; and the leaves of the tree were for the healing of the nations.'[10]

Whatever human imagery is offered for capturing heavenly hopes, it needs constant refreshment to keep it alive. Good news is notoriously harder to make interesting than bad news. Even Dante's visit to paradise is not as memorable nor indeed as popular as his tour of hell. It takes multiple overlapping finite pictures to add up to three-dimensional encouragement about infinite hopes. Among many favourite images of heaven, there is one in particular which is more authoritative than most and which is capable of including a good deal of variety within itself. This is the image of the celestial feast which recurs so repeatedly in the Gospels.

It is time to bring together some scattered indications of where this line of thought has been heading. The upshot is that whatever else the Christian faith affirms, near its heart is the idea of welcome.[11] To be *someone* in the sight of God is to be wanted as a member of God's family, with a place prepared ready for one's longed-for arrival. Homecoming is a basic biblical notion, whether the emphasis is on the people of God returning from exile, or on the good Shepherd rescu-

---

[9] Rudyard Kipling: 'Sussex'.
[10] *Revelation* 22.1–2.
[11] See above, pp. 100, 103, 136,156, 185; and especially p. 168.

ing the lost sheep who has gone astray, or on God's family gathering where they rightly belong.

There is more to the image of welcome than 'Welcome home'. Though in the end God's children are to find that heaven is the place where they belong, they must also keep saying, just as firmly, that it is not by right but by God's grace that people can hope to enter there. They have the honour of being invited to the heavenly banquet as chosen guests. This Christian hope of God's welcome does not depend on an argument from proof-texts, but on the composite picture of the Lord's characteristic teaching which emerges from all the Gospels.[12]

Making people welcome is an especially promising image for connecting Christian lives now with their hopes of what they may find at their journey's end. Hospitality is a theme which is picked up throughout the New Testament.[13] It is particularly encouraging, because it is a dynamic not a static idea. To take up this biblical way of imagining heaven can allow Christians to put aside one persistent notion of eternal life which some people find more alarming than promising. It is hard to look forward eagerly to a state of affairs where everyone is fixed for ever, kneeling in unchanging devotion or resting in endless peace. The idea that the welcome awaiting us is lively and variegated is more hopeful. What hospitality provides is refreshment and entertainment, carefully prepared and warmly offered. The pleasure given is meant to be spirited and reciprocal

Hosts and guests are present for each other's sake. According to Marilyn McCord Adams, 'at the marriage feast of the Lamb, we will eat and drink with God in a literally shared meal'.[14] In the Gospel parables this recurrent image of the Kingdom of heaven as a feast celebrating a marriage encourages Christians to hope for a heaven where

[12]   See above, p. 168, and *Romans* 15.7.
[13]   e.g. *Romans* 12:.3; *1 Timothy* 3.2; *Titus* 1.8; *1 Peter* 4.9; see Oppenheimer (1988), p. 148.
[14]   Adams (2006), p. 237.

people will go on from a good beginning to a maturing and fruitful happiness.[15]

Those Christians who are natural non-conformists, who dislike being stereotyped themselves and who are glad of the multiplicity and variety of their fellow creatures, need not fear that God's invited guests will have to conform to one set pattern. They can be heartened by the Lord's saying in the Fourth Gospel, 'In my Father's house are many mansions: if it were not so, I would have told you. I go to prepare a place for you.'[16] Translating 'mansions' nowadays as 'rooms',[17] individualists can take hold of the idea that since each person is special, the place made ready for each person will likewise be special.

Damnation still has a dreadful meaning, but not a sadistic one.[18] If anyone has to be excluded from heaven, it is by refusing the invitation and turning away from the welcome. Staying crossly outside is a negative attitude which Jesus evidently condemned.[19] If anybody must be positively cast out, it will be the hard-hearted ones whose stubborn ungratefulness would wreck the gathering for the other guests.

The biblical accounts of the Lord's teaching do include fearful threats of rejection, but too often the wrong people take them to heart. Pious people torment themselves that they may have committed the sin against the Holy Spirit which will never be forgiven,[20] forgetting that the Holy Spirit is not God angrily confronting us but God within, enlightening us. To sin against the Holy Spirit is not an offence which someone might commit inadvertently. To turn one's back on grace and to shut out inspiration would be a way of becoming a spiritual black hole.

It is not a debating point to keep pointing out that Gehenna was not a dungeon but a rubbish dump outside Jerusalem. Rubbish is burnt or rotted away, not imprisoned

---

[15] cf. Gregory of Nyssa on growth in goodness, quoted above, p. 201.
[16] *John* 14.2 King James Version.
[17] ibid. *Revised Standard Version*.
[18] See above, p. 191.
[19] e.g. *Luke* 15. 25–32.
[20] *Matthew* 12.31; see Oppenheimer (1995/2003), p. 66.

for life and locked up eternally. Some Christians always cherish the hope that even if there has to be a gloomy hell outside the boundaries of heaven, it will eventually be unoccupied, because God's love will persist until every living soul can be welcomed back into the light.[21]

Still more welcoming than a reserved place is a feast set out all ready for one's coming. The invitation to the heavenly celebration offers the enticements of nourishment and good company. People who heartily believe that their unworthiness really will be forgiven and put behind them can allow an element of fun and frivolity into their pictures of heaven, which surely would do some solemn Christians good. The Host at this joyful party is the Lord who was called a gluttonous man and a winebibber[22] and who was a welcome guest of worldly people.[23]

A main meaning of the Christian Eucharist is a foretaste of the heavenly feast. It would be a shame to let the pious meaning of the Host as not a person but a wafer take over the thinking of church people. If Catholic or Protestant Christians think of this Thanksgiving as the performance of a prescribed ceremony, duly enacted for the proper worship of God, they may suppose that the Lord must be especially located in that particular consecrated object which is the distinctive component of the rite. But when the congregation say together, 'The Lord is here', they are responding to the encouraging welcome of Someone who is calling them to come to a celebration.

Christians interpret this sacrament of theirs in multiple positive ways. For some, what matters is that the Eucharist is a sacrifice. For others, it is more like a memorial service. Whatever theory people find most illuminating, they would do well to argue less and use their imaginations more, so that they could take pleasure in their ritual eating and drinking together as a faithful response to God's heavenly invitation. They can hope to find the *real presence* of Christ, welcoming and feeding the companions who have

---

[21] See Robinson (1950); Oppenheimer (1988), p. 132.
[22] *Matthew* 11.19 / *Luke* 7.34.
[23] e.g. *Luke* 5.29–30; 19.5–6; also *Matthew* 9.10; *Mark* 2.15–16.

gathered in his name.[24] 'Com*pan*ion' means 'bread-sharer'.
When Christians break bread together, one meaning of
their ritual is that they are accepting the Lord's invitation.
Christians who 'do this' can look back to the stories of Jesus
sharing meals with his disciples, not concentrating only on
the Last Supper, and with all this in mind they can be encouraged to look forward to the promised heavenly festival.[25]

Meantime in this life the Eucharist is a *means of grace*, a
source of blessing, available for nourishing the people of
God. The sacrament is based on actual eating and drinking,
because eating and drinking is the best image of spiritual
nourishment for human beings who are bodily creatures
needing real food to sustain them. The bread really is for
strengthening and the wine really is for gladdening the
human heart.[26] The physical and the spiritual are not to be
taken apart. When St Paul rebuked the Corinthians celebrating the Lord's supper for letting their social divisions
spoil their hospitality, some going hungry and some getting
drunk,[27] it was their ordinary human greed which showed
how they were missing the spiritual point. They were
failing to see or show that at the service where Christians
give thanks over bread and wine their real physical eating
and drinking with one another provide the spiritual nourishment to build up the Body of Christ.

To offer the pleasures of human entertainment as an
image of eternal life could seem trivial, worldly, or even
selfish, but the image is worth defending and commending.
Hospitality throughout most of human history has been
much more important than a fashionable dinner party. To
welcome strangers has been acknowledged as a sacred
duty. To eat people's bread is to recognize them morally. To
neglect or mistreat a guest is an offence not only mean but
disgraceful. It would seem that a dire failure of hospitality

---

[24] See Wells (2006), Part 3, e.g. p. 128.
[25] See Oppenheimer (1994), e.g. pp. 129–31, 149–50.
[26] *Psalm* 104.15
[27] *1 Corinthians* 11.21.

was the sin of the inhabitants of Sodom, whose shock-waves are still felt today.[28]

Extravagant overflowing provision, which does honour to guest and host, offers a vivid analogy for the superlative grace of God. Gallons of vintage wine are made available for a country wedding.[29] Killing the fatted calf is not too lavish a reception for an unruly son who has eventually come home.[30]

This image of welcome, biblically rooted though it is, cannot be reserved as the special property of a devout in-group. People across the centuries have practised hospitality in ways we still understand. All manner of people can and do join, one way and another, in the familiar activity of being hosts and guests. Hospitality is a kind of art form, in which the artist's values are by no means at odds with moral values, but united in the same concern to exercise skills both everyday and excellent.

The ordinary customs of making welcome belong to our fundamental humanity, all the way from classical heroes feasting on roast meat with libations; to monastery guest-houses receiving travellers; to Jane Austen's Fanny Price, who wore a white dress with glossy spots at her first grown-up party; to John Betjeman's self-conscious hostess who was concerned whether trifle was 'sufficient for sweet'; to a neighbour who has dropped in for a cup of tea and a biscuit; to the children's party where the birthday girl invites the whole class and each child has a party bag to take home. All these people are variously putting into practice comprehensible human ideals of what hospitality should mean.

Human traditions are full of descriptions of hospitality as responsibility and as blessing. Ancient Greeks told the story of Philemon and Baucis, who found that the strangers they had welcomed were the great gods Zeus and Hermes. Abraham reverently attended to his unexpected guests[31] and

---

[28]   *Genesis* 19.1–8.
[29]   *John* 2. 1–11.
[30]   *Luke* 15.11–32.
[31]   *Genesis* 18.1–10.

thereby entertained the Almighty unawares.[32] The Jewish Passover meal is not a ceremony in charge of a presiding priest but a family gathering, where the youngest child is given the ritual task of asking what this festivity means.

Hospitality is a concept wide-reaching enough to offer all manner of pictures of human and divine celebration. The ancient and modern ways in which human beings set about looking after their guests and making them welcome suggest the most promising images of the heavenly welcome which Christians believe God has prepared for everyone. However naive these hopes seem to sceptics, and however childish these human pictures surely appear in God's eyes, the encouragement they offer is more than fanciful storytelling. The conviction of Christians is biblical and basic, that earthly life is not the only life and that in God's kingdom there are 'pleasures for evermore'.[33]

Further reading

Adams, Marilyn McCord (2006) *Christ and horrors*. Cambridge University Press: Chapter 8 'Resurrection and renewal'.

Oppenheimer, Helen (1983) *The hope of happiness*. SCM Press: Chapters 19 and 20.

Oppenheimer, Helen (1990) 'Spirit and body', *Theology* March/April.

Oppenheimer, Helen (1994) *Finding & following*. SCM Press: Chapters 16 and 17

Robinson, J.A.T. (1950) *In the End, God*. James Clarke.

Wells, Samuel (2006) *God's companions; re-imagining Christian ethics*. Blackwells.

---

[32] *Hebrews* 13.2.
[33] *Psalm* 16.12.

References

Adams, Marilyn McCord (2006) *Christ and horrors*. Cambridge University Press.

Allchin, A.M. (1978), *The world is a wedding*. Darton, Longman & Todd.

Atkinson, J.D. and D.H. Field, ed. (1995) *New dictionary of Christian ethics and pastoral theology*. InterVarsity Press.

Austin, John (1962) *How to do things with words*. Oxford University Press.

Avramides, Anita (2001) *Other minds* in series The problems of philosophy. Routledge.

Badham, Paul (2009) *Is there a Christian case for assisted dying?* SPCK.

Baillie, John (1934) *And the life everlasting*. OUP.

Baker, John Austin (1970) *The foolishness of God*. Darton, Longman & Todd.

Baron-Cohen, Simon, Helen Tager-Flusberg & Donald J. Cohen, eds (1993) *Understanding other minds: perspectives from autism*. Oxford Medical Publications.

Barr, James (1992) *The garden of Eden and the hope of immortality*. SCM Press.

Bauckham, Richard (1997) 'Jesus the revelation of God' in *Divine revelation*, ed. Paul Avis. Darton, Longman & Todd.

Bauckham, Richard (2006) *Jesus and the eyewitnesses*. Eerdmans.

Bentham, Jeremy (1789) *Introduction to the principles of morals and legislation*.

Biggar, Nigel (2004) *Aiming to kill*. Darton, Longman & Todd.

Brooks, D.H.M. (1988) 'Dogs and slaves', *Proceedings of the Aristotelian Society*.

Buber, Martin (1923) *Ich und du* (English translation *I and thou* 1937).

Buford, Thomas O., ed (1970) *Essays on other minds*. University of Illinois Press.

Butler, Joseph (1726) Preface to *Fifteen Sermons preached at the Rolls Chapel*.

Butler, Joseph (1729) Dissertation: 'Of the nature of virtue' Section 13.

Castelo, Daniel (2008) 'Moltmann's dismissal of divine impassibility' *Scottish journal of theology* 2008:4.

Castelo, Daniel (2009) *The apathetic God: exploring the contemporary relevance of divine impassibility*. Paternoster Theological Monographs

Chambers biographical dictionary (1990), ed. Magnus Magnusson.

Clark, S.R.L. (1997) *Animals and their moral standing*. Cambridge University Press.

Cook, E.D. (1995) 'Abortion' in Atkinson and Field (1995).

Cook Wilson, J. (1926) 'Rational grounds of belief in God' in *Statement and inference* Vol. II. Oxford University Press.

Creel, Richard E. (1986) *Divine impassibility: An essay in philosophical theology*. Cambridge University Press.

Creel, Richard E.(1997) 'Immutability and impassibility' in *A companion to philosophy of religion*. Blackwell.

Cullmann, Oscar (1958) *Immortality of the soul or resurrection of the dead?* Epworth Press.

de Waal, Frans (1996) *Good natured: the origins of right and wrong in humans and other animals*. Harvard University Press.

Dunstan, G.R. (1962) *The family is not broken*. SCM Press.

Dunstan, G.R. (1974) *The artifice of ethics*. SCM Press.

Dunstan, G.R., ed. (1990) *The human embryo: Aristotle and the Arabic and European traditions*, the report of the Constantinus Colloquy, a multi-disciplinary conference held at Exeter University in 1988. University of Exeter Press.

Emmet, Dorothy (1966) *Rules, roles and relations*. Macmillan.

Farrer, A.M. (1948) *The glass of vision*. Dacre Press.

Farrer, Austin (1964) *Saving belief*. Hodder & Stoughton.

Farrer, Austin (1970) 'For a marriage' in *A celebration of faith*. Hodder & Stoughton.

Fiddes, Paul (1988) *The creative suffering of God* 1988 Clarendon paperbacks.

Fiddes, Paul (2001) 'Creation out of love' in *The work of love: creation as kenosis*, ed. John Polkinghorne. SPCK.

Flew, Anthony (1955) 'Theology and falsification' in *New essays in philosophical theology*, ed. Flew and MacIntyre. SCM Press.

Ford, N.M. (1988) *When did I begin?* Cambridge University Press.

Gavrilyuk, Paul L. (2004) *The suffering of the impassible God*. Oxford Early Christian Studies.

Gavrilyuk, Paul L. (2009) 'God's impassible suffering in the flesh' in *Divine impassibility and the mystery of human suffering*, ed. Keating and White. Eerdmann.

Goodall, Jane (1988) *In the shadow of man*, revised edition. Phoenix paperback.

Goodrich, T. (1969) 'The morality of killing', *Philosophy* 44: 127–139.

Habgood, J. (1993) *Making sense*. SPCK.

Habgood, J. (1998) *Being a person: Where faith and science meet*. Darton, Longman & Todd.

Hare, R.M. (1952) *The language of morals*. Clarendon Press.

Harries, Richard (2010), *Questions of life and death: Christian faith and medical intervention*. SPCK.

Hart, H.L.A. (1962) *The concept of law*. Oxford University Press.

Hearne, Vicki (1986) *Adam's task*. Heinemann.

Hick, John, ed. (1977) *The myth of God incarnate*. SCM Press.

Hobson, Peter (1993) 'Understanding persons: The role of affect' in Baron-Cohen *et al.* (1993).

Hume, David (1740) *A treatise of human nature* Book III Part 1, end of Section i.

Jenkins, David (1976) *The contradiction of Christianity*. SCM Press.

Julian of Norwich (1978) *Showings*, Classics of western spirituality. Paulist Press.

Keating, James F. and Thomas Joseph White, ed. (2009) *Divine impassibility and the mystery of human suffering*. Eerdmann.

Lewis, C.S. (1942) *Screwtape Letters*. Geoffrey Bles. Many editions.

Lewis, C.S. (1952) *Mere Christianity*. Geoffrey Bles. Many editions.

Lewis, C.S. (1962) *They Asked for a Paper: Papers and Addresses*. Geoffrey Bles.

Lorenz, Konrad (1966) *On aggression* English edition, Methuen.

Lovejoy, Arthur O. (1953) *The great chain of being: a study of an idea*. Harvard University Press.

Macmurray, John (1961) *Persons in relation*. Faber & Faber.

Meltzoff, Andrew and Alison Gopnik (1993) 'The role of imitation in understanding persons and developing a theory of mind' in Baron-Cohen *et al.* (1993).

Midgley, Mary (2006) 'On Dover Beach' *Philosophy*, April.

Moltmann, Jürgen (1974) *The crucified God*, trans. John Bowden and R.A. Wilson. SCM Press.

Moore, G.E. (1929) *Principia ethica*. Cambridge University Press.

Muir, Edwin (1960) *Collected poems 1921–58*. Faber & Faber.

Nagel, Thomas (1979) 'What is it like to be a bat?' in *Mortal questions* Cambridge University Press.

Nagel, Thomas (1986) *The view from nowhere*. Oxford University Press.

Nuttall, A.D. (2007) *Shakespeare the thinker*. Yale University Press.

Oppenheimer, Helen (1970) 'Head and members' in *The sacred ministry* ed. G.R. Dunstan.

Oppenheimer, Helen (1971) 'Marriage as illustrating some Christian doctrines' Appendix 4 to *Marriage, Divorce and the church*, The report of the Commission on the Christian doctrine of marriage. SPCK.

Oppenheimer, Helen with Hugh Montefiore (1971) 'Vows', appendix to *Marriage, divorce and the church,* The report of the Commission on the Christian doctrine of marriage. SPCK.

Oppenheimer, Helen (1973) *Incarnation and immanence*. Hodder & Stoughton.

Oppenheimer, Helen (1975) 'Ought and is' in *Duty and discernment*, ed. G.R. Dunstan. SCM Press (Reprinted from *Theology* June 1965).

Oppenheimer, Helen (1978) 'Fidelity' The Mary Sumner Lecture 1978.

Oppenheimer, Helen (1983) *The hope of happiness*. SCM Press.

Oppenheimer, Helen (1988) *Looking before and after* (The Archbishop of Canterbury's Lent Book). Collins Fount.

Oppenheimer, Helen (1988a) 'Making God findable' in *The parish church*, ed. Giles Ecclestone. The Grubb Institute.

Oppenheimer, Helen (1989) 'Handling life' in *Doctors' decisions*, ed. G.R. Dunstan and E. A. Shinebourne. Oxford University Press.

Oppenheimer, Helen (1990) 'Spirit and body', *Theology* March/April.

Oppenheimer, Helen (1991) 'Belonging and the individual'; *TRUST*, a newsletter of SCM Press Trust No.5.

Oppenheimer, Helen (1991a) 'Blessing' in *The weight of glory: Essays for Peter Baelz*, ed. D.W. Hardy and P.H. Sedgwick. T. & T. Clark.

Oppenheimer, Helen (1992) 'Abortion: A sketch for a Christian view', *Journal of Christian ethics* 5:2.

Oppenheimer, Helen (1994) *Finding & following*. SCM Press.

Oppenheimer, Helen (1995/2003) 'Mattering, *Studies in Christian ethics*, 8:1 (reprinted in *Approaches to ethics nursing beyond boundaries* ed. Verena Tschudin. Butterworth Heinemann).

Oppenheimer, Helen (1995) 'Remembering', *Theology* November/December.

Oppenheimer, Helen (2000) 'The truth-telling animal' in *Dumbing down*, ed. Ivo Mosley. Imprint Academic.

Oppenheimer, Helen (2001) *Making good*. SCM Press.

Oppenheimer, Helen (2006) *What a piece of work*. Imprint Academic.

Otto, Rudof (1923) *The idea of the holy*. Oxford University Press.

Oxford companion to the mind (1987), ed. Richard Gregory. Oxford University Press.

Oxford dictionary of the Christian church, 3rd edition (1997), ed. F.L. Cross & E.A. Livingsone. Oxford University Press.

Parfit, Derek (1985) *Reasons and persons*. Clarendon Press.

Peart-Binns, John (2007) *A heart in my head: A biography of Richard Harries*. Continuum.

Polkinghorne, John, ed. (2001) *The work of love: creation as kenosis*. SPCK.

Price, H.H. (1932) 'Our knowledge of other minds', *Proceedings of the Aristotelian Society* Vol. XXXII. See also Buford (1970).

Regan, Tom (2004) *The case for animal rights*, updated version. University of California Press.

Robinson, J.A.T. (1950) *In the End, God*. James Clarke.

Robinson, J.A.T. (1952) *The body: A study in Pauline theology*, Studies in biblical theology No.5. SCM Press.

Rolf, Sibille (2010) Review of Paul Badham *Is there a Christian case for assisted dying?*, *Theology*, March 2010, p. 153.

Rupp, G. (1953) *The righteousness of God*. Hodder.

Ryle, Gilbert (1949) *The concept of mind*. Hutchinson.

Sacks, Jonathan (2004) 'Political society, civil society' in *Values, education and the human world*, ed. John Haldane. Imprint Academic.

Sharpe, Lynne (2005) *Creatures like us*. Imprint Academic.

Squire, J.C. (1926) *Poems in one volume*. Heinemann.

Stackhouse, Max L. (2007) 'Vocation' in *The Oxford handbook of theological ethics*, pp. 189–190.

Strawson, Peter (1959) *Individuals*. Methuen.

Thomson, J.J. (1971) 'A defense of abortion', *Philosophy and public affairs*, 1:1.

Thompson, Marianne Meye (2000) *The promise of the Father*. Westminster John Knox Press.

Tolley, George (2008) '"Love was his meaning": Julian of Norwich and atonement', *Theology*, March/April.

Traherne, Thomas (1960) *Centuries* . Faith Press.

VandenBerg, M. (2007) 'Redemptive suffering: Christ's alone', Scottish Journal of Theology 60 (4), pp. 394–411.

Vanstone, W.H. (1977) *God's endeavour, God's expense*. DLT.

Warnock Report (1984) *Report of the Committee of enquiry into human fertilisation and embryology*. Her Majesty's Stationery Office.

Warnock, Mary & Elisabeth Macdonald (2008) *Easeful death: Is there a case for assisted dying?* Oxford University Press.

Webb, C.C.J. (1911) *Divine personality and human life: Problems in the relations of God and man* Nisbet.

Webb, C.C.J. (1918) *God and personality*, Gifford Lectures vol. 1. George Allen.

Webb, C.C.J. (1919) *Divine personality and human life* , Gifford Lectures vol. 2. George Allen.

Weinandy, Thomas G. (2000) *Does God suffer?* T & T Clark.

Wells, Samuel (2006) *God's companions; re-imagining Christian ethics*. Blackwells.

Whitehead, A.N. (1978) *Process and reality*, 3rd ed. The Free Press.

Williams, Bernard (1961) 'Moral luck,' *Proceedings of the Aristotelian Society* Supplementary Vol. L (Reprinted in *Moral luck: Philosophical papers 1973–1980* Cambridge University Press).

Williams, Bernard (1973) 'Personal identity and individuation' in *Problems of the self*. Cambridge University Press.

Williams, Bernard (1986) Review of Strawson, *Philosophy*, 61, p. 332.

Wittgenstein, L. (1953) *Philosophical investigations*. Blackwell.

Woodward, James (2008) *Reviews in Religion & theology*, 15: 1, pp. 47–50.

Indexes

Index of Biblical References

Index of Proper Names